Triathlon

NH
NEW
HOLLAND
MIKE FINCH

First published in 2004 by New Holland Publishers
London • Cape Town • Sydney • Auckland
www.newhollandpublishers.com
86 Edgware Road, London, W2 2EA, United Kingdom
80 McKenzie Street, Cape Town, 8001, South Africa
14 Aquatic Drive, Frenchs Forest, NSW 2086, Australia
218 Lake Road, Northcote, Auckland, New Zealand

ISBN 1 84330 362 0 (hardcover)
ISBN 1 84330 363 9 (softcover)

Publisher and editor: Mariëlle Renssen
Commissioning editor: Ingrid Corbett
Publishing managers: Claudia dos Santos, Simon Pooley
Concept and design: Sheryl Buckley
Illustrations: Angus Cameron
Picture research: Karla Kik
Proofreader: Annlerie van Rooyen
Indexer: Leizel Brown
Production: Myrna Collins
Consultants: **Graeme Maw PHD**, PERFORMANCE DIRECTOR, BRITISH TRIATHLON ASSOCIATION;
BJ Hoeptner Evans, USA TRIATHLON COMMUNICATIONS AND MEDIA RELATIONS DIRECTOR

Reproduction by Hirt & Carter (Pty) Ltd, Cape Town
Printed and bound in Malaysia by Times Offset (M) Sdn Bhd
10 9 8 7 6 5 4 3 2

contents

I don't remember the first real book about triathlon. It must not have left a mark on me; or maybe I was somehow satisfied to stay within the exploratory milieu that was the sport in its early days. After all, you couldn't make any money off it, the races themselves were a rare occurrence, and if you happened to mention to a friend that you had done a triathlon, he asked how many days it had taken. Somewhere along the way we were discovered – or I should say, people found that the sport could help them discover themselves. The sport grew up without technical how-to's and multimedia instruction; but it didn't grow too far.

Triathlon is not an easy sport. At certain levels, it requires things that most sports don't even acknowledge. Like the tendency to be obsessive-compulsive; like a very deep-seated knowledge of why the hell you're out there beating yourself up every day. Therein lies the irony. Somewhere else along the way, about the same time people started to dissect the intricacies of the sport and write books about it, triathletes figured out some simple yet monumental discoveries. Like more is not better; that you could sample the beneficial fruit of this quirky triple sport and still walk down stairs without oohing and aahing in pain with each step. There are days when I consider how little we knew about cycling back then – I laugh until I feel the weight of lost opportunity and naiveté. Who knew? We did the best we could.

The documentation of knowledge put a more easing, didactic angle on triathlon. You didn't have to read everything to improve, but if you were interested in shortcutting the vast mistakes we made in 1975 and 1980, and were still making in 1985, you had the manual in front of you. Books didn't really change the sport – not like drafting or triple-figure entry fees. But they sure helped a lot of people get closer to finding what they were looking for out there on the trails and roads that defined the world's training grounds. And as new people discover the sport all the time, books provide that service.

So along comes yet another book on triathlon – this time from a place that may not have the reputation of San Diego, California, or Boulder, Colorado, but that may, in fact, be an undiscovered beauty lying waiting, goggles and shoes in hand. Michael Finch has penned a comprehensive look at the sport from the best view possible: the inside looking out. He has given triathletes an excellent overview of much of what they need: not only to improve at the sport but also to have a good time doing so. And shouldn't that be the goal?

Good reading, safe training.

SCOTT TINLEY

Del Mar, California, USA

1 INTRODUCTION

I started with triathlon out of necessity. I'd been a runner most of my life, but as my aspirations in running – and increased mileage – soared, so did my list of injuries. It was then I met a real triathlete – Joe – at the local running club time-trial. He was the epitome of the body perfect: shaved, tanned, with defined legs, and strong but lean arms. I wanted to look like that.

It wasn't long before I'd bought my first bicycle and tentatively stroked out my first few lengths in the local council pool. It gave me a new lease on my running life. Suddenly I could train more without getting injured, my running improved because of the cross training and my skinny body began to gradually morph into a more muscular version of my former self.

It took me a full year to get up the courage to actually attempt my first triathlon. The swim scared me and I was intimidated by the many Joe lookalikes who sauntered around the transition zone before races. When I finally pulled off my maiden triathlon finish, it transformed my life. I could finally call myself 'a triathlete' and it gave me an indescribable inner sense of achievement. Yes, there were swimmers who swam faster, cyclists who cycled better and runners who ran swifter, but I could do what many of them couldn't – all three in one event.

It didn't take long for me to go the whole hog. I'd whimper at the local salon as my wife's beautician waxed my legs free of hair, I maxed-out the credit card on a decent tri bike and most mornings were spent with Joe and his swim squad sweating blood in the local health club pool.

Ten years down the line, that passion has got stronger and has culminated in this book, *Triathlon*.

It is packed with everything I wish I knew 10 years ago, from the basics of the triathlon to training for an Ironman event. For those already part of this 'tri' world, I have delved deeper and picked the brains of some of the world's top athletes and coaches to discover their myriad secrets. I began this book with the ambition of turning out 'the best darned triathlon book in the world'. I hope I have succeeded.

SPEEDO
ST. CROIX
ST. CROIX
MERICA
EXPRE

ORIGINS AND ORACLES

Triathlon started like many modern sports – as an offshoot of more established disciplines, honed into a hybrid that gradually attracts a new, unique band of disciples. It is unlikely that any one individual can claim the rights to being the inventor of the triathlon. In the early 1970s swimmers, cyclists, canoeists and runners in southern California found themselves challenging each other in various multi-disciplined events. Early reports suggested that swim-run biathlons were the embryonic stage of the triathlon, although triathlon historians claim that it was bike-swim and run-swim races that first became the litmus paper for this particular sport. There is little doubt that it was the motivation behind completing a multidisciplined event that had much to do with the advent of triathlon; even in the early days, athletes who were competent in more than one sport would often be seen as 'fringe players' – superfit madmen eager to take on a tougher challenge.

While many believe that the first triathlon was the inaugural Hawaii Ironman competition in 1978, credit should go to two San Diegans, Jack Johnstone and Don Shanahan, for organizing the first swim-cycle-run triathlon. The event took in a 2.8-mile run, a 5-mile bicycle ride, a quarter-mile swim – and ended with another 2-mile run and quarter-mile swim (4.5km; 8km; 400m; 3.2km; 400m)!

Johnstone was first introduced to the world of multidisciplined sport at the age of 35 when he was swept up in the jogging craze that hit the USA in the early 1970s. A good collegiate swimmer in his youth, Johnstone had a competitive streak and was eager to relive this success – but running was clearly not it. He then heard about David Pain's Birthday Biathlon, an annual run-swim event that was due to be staged in 1973 for the second time. The run was 4.5 miles and the swim a quarter-mile (7.2km; 400m) long, but for Johnstone it was an ideal opportunity to improve his success rating. He finished among the top 20 in his first event, then crept into the top 10 the following year.

Bitten by the bug, Johnstone decided to organize his own event, to include more swimming and involve multiple disciplines. With the help of the San Diego Track Club he was introduced to Don Shanahan, who suggested adding a cycle leg. Although not overly excited at the prospect of adding this unknown activity, Johnstone finally agreed and the Mission Bay Triathlon was finally set for 25 September 1974.

Origin of the word

Jack Johnstone can probably lay claim to being the first person to organize a triathlon with his Mission Bay event, and he can definitely be credited with devising the term 'triathlon'. Unsure of how to spell the word when his trophy-maker first asked for it, Johnstone simply adapted the term from established sports like pentathlon, heptathlon and decathlon.

'Ironman' is born

As is the case with any success story, one thing led to another, although it took some four years to happen, on the island of Hawaii. One of the Mission Bay finishers was a certain John Collins who finished 35th in his first attempt. For Collins, it was the seed that would grow into an event which would ultimately put the sport of triathlon firmly on the map. John Collins's story is well known but worth repeating for its romanticism.

Fours years after the Mission Bay triathlon, Collins, as a US Navy Commander, found himself stationed in Hawaii. On one fateful night, Collins and a group of fellow fitness friends found themselves arguing over whether swimmers, cyclists or runners were the fitter sports-people. A visionary by nature, Collins proposed a single-day event that would take in the Waikiki Rough Water Swim over 2.4 miles, the 112-mile Around Oahu Bike Race and end with a run along the entire 26.2-mile Honolulu Marathon course (3.9km; 180km; 42.2km).

Still today there are many hardened fitness fanatics who stare disbelievingly at the suggestion that anyone could manage such a race in one day. But on 18 February 1978, 15 like-minded men took to the Pacific Ocean in compliance with Collins's suggestion. He had manufactured a crude trophy made from iron and bent into the shape of a man, and it was decided that the winner would henceforth be known as the 'ironman'.

Ironman's first winner

Taxi driver Gordon Haller was the winner of the first Ironman triathlon. He finished the 2.4-mile swim, 112-mile bike ride and 26.2-mile run in 11 hours and 46 minutes. If Haller had finished in the same time in 2001, he would have finished second last in the elite section of the Hawaii Ironman of that year!

OPPOSITE TOP *Runners take part in the London Marathon in 1908. Just over 70 years later, the jogging craze would contribute to the start of triathlon.*

ABOVE LEFT *The Hawaii Ironman was the first triathlon event to get television coverage, which succeeded in popularizing the sport. It has retained its status as the ultimate test of endurance to this day*

INSPIRING MODERN TRIATHLETES

Julie Moss

If Johnstone and Collins are to be recognized as triathlon's inventors, then Californian Julie Moss will go down as the sport's first real celebrity. Although US television network ABC had already taken cameras to previous Ironman events to film this 'extreme' challenge, it was Moss who grabbed public attention in 1982 in the Hawaii World Championships when she stumbled, fell and crawled her way to second place.

The ordeal of the petite athlete's desperate bid for the line was beamed into millions of US homes and was made even more dramatic when Kathleen McCartney passed Moss in the final stretch to take victory. Moss's courage may have looked like demented masochism to some, but for many it was an inspiration – a chance that they, too, possibly had the determination and guts that Moss displayed.

Mark Allen

One of those who sat riveted while Moss crawled was Mark Allen. Like many his first reaction was one of amazement at how people could do this to themselves. But the allure of challenging the body to such extremes was too high, and by the following year he had trained hard enough to enter the race himself. His story is that of a classic Ironman fairytale: an ordinary man suddenly drawn to an extraordinary event.

In his first triathlon in 1983, the American finished third to begin an Ironman career that would catapult him into sporting folklore. Allen would compete another five times before he won in Hawaii, but when he finally beat his nemesis, Dave Scott, in 1989, it produced one of the greatest triathlon races in history. Scott, who had won six races since 1980, looked unbeatable until that year, but Allen trained like a man possessed. The two athletes hit the final marathon leg running side by side, and for those lucky enough to witness the smooth flowing style of Allen up against the more ungainly amble of Scott, it was the ultimate race. Allen eventually pulled clear up the final hill – and for the next six years, he would prove almost invincible, losing only once in 1994.

Spreading the word

The media attention and the celebrity status that men like Allen and Scott created began to expose the sport of triathlon around the world. Shorter events were held and unofficial world championships were staged over various distances throughout the 1980s. With the establishment of the International Triathlon Union (ITU), the sport became more organized, and in 1989 the first official World Championships were held in Avignon, France – a country that had embraced the sport from early on.

The race distance of a 1500m swim, 40km cycle and 10km run (0.9 mile; 25 miles; 6.2 miles) is now recognized as the standard, or Olympic, distance in triathlon. Mark Allen won the men's race and New Zealand's Erin Baker the women's, as triathletes from almost 40 countries took part. Cleverly, the ITU made sure that they continued to spread the word by staging the championships in every corner of the world. In 1990, they were held in Disney World, USA; in 1991 at the Gold Coast in Australia; and in 1992 in Canada.

As triathlon began to mature, so did the athletes. While Allen, Dave Scott and Paula Newby-Fraser dominated the long-distance events, men like Simon Lessing, Spencer Smith and Chris McCormack and women like Michellie Jones, Emma Carney and Karen Smyers began to make names for themselves over the shorter distances.

The sport struck a chord in countries like Australia and France, and events of many varying distances were organized backed by big sponsors. In Australia, the Mrs T's Sprint Series brought together some of the world's best in an early-season event that included a series of short, sharp legs over multiple laps. The focus was on spectator value – something that the sport had been sadly lacking.

ABOVE RIGHT *The introduction of Olympic-distance triathlon racing led to its rapid inclusion on the world's premier sporting stage – the Olympics themselves.*

The drafting controversy

Perhaps the biggest change in the sport came in 1996, when the International Triathlon Union, eager to make the sport more television friendly, took the decision to make their international World Cup events draft (draught) legal: in other words, the elite triathletes, previously prevented from drafting behind other competitors on the bike leg, could now do so. As far as the purists were concerned, the decision was a 'selling out' of triathlon's soul. The event suddenly became a tactical one that favoured strong swimmers and runners, instead of an individual test of pure physical ability. There is little doubt, though, that it aided triathlon's bid to become an Olympic sport, a goal that ITU president Les McDonald had been lobbying for since the early 1990s. It all paid off in 2000, when triathlon finally made its Olympic debut in front of an estimated audience of four billion and produced two outstanding races – Canadian Simon Whitfield and Swiss Brigitte McMahon took the wins. No other sport had achieved Olympic status in such a short time frame. The sport as it is today is run by 107 federations around the world attracting millions of devotees – the advantages of multidisciplined sport seem to be finding a place in the lives of single-sport diehards.

TRIATHLON TRAINING: BASIC PRINCIPLES

Set a goal

As with any sport, the only true way of maintaining motivation is to set yourself a goal. This can be both long and short term. The goal is usually a race, but you can set goals within your training that will help you achieve a long-term plan, e.g. if your long-term goal is to race a Sprint Distance (Half Standard), your short-term plan will be to successfully swim 750m (0.5 mile) in a pool in a goal time, do a time trial on a bicycle for 20km (12 miles) or run a set time for a 5km (3 miles) run. For the more experienced, you can use smaller races as short-terms goals, as part of your preparation for a long-term goal. When you're planning any goal, work backwards from the date of the event in your logbook and plan your build-up that way. Without a goal, training will be unfocused and, inevitably, unsuccessful.

Find a friend

In a sport as demanding as triathlon, it's important to find training partners. First prize is a partner of similar ability. Training partners help to get you out of bed on cold mornings and they motivate; without them, triathlon can be a lonely sport.

Reality rules

Top US running coach and *Runner's World* contributor Bobby McGee is a strong advocate for being realistic about your goals. When designing a training programme, keep in mind all the other parts of your life that are likely to be influenced, including your family commitments, your job and your social life. Once you have worked out how much time you can truly commit to training, you can then set realistic, and achievable, goals.

10% training

During training, the cardiovascular system adapts far quicker than the muscles, ligaments and tendons. It's therefore easy to do too much, too soon.

Make sure you only increase the time (and therefore distance) you devote to each discipline every week by 10%, for a safe, injury-free build-up.

Consistency counts

Half an hour every day is far better than one hour every second day. Sure, every training programme needs a rest day, but it is more important to train consistently than to throw in big training sessions once in a while to 'make up', as consistence builds endurance and strength.

Real rest

Believe it or not, lack of recovery is the biggest mistake made by experienced and novice triathletes alike. Once you get hooked in by the endorphin rush of training and the desire to become as fit as possible, it is easy to convince yourself that you can go without a complete rest day. On the contrary, a rest day once a week not only allows the body to get stronger, but is also a vital mental break.

Fabulous fun

The key to success in any sport is the degree of enjoyment you gain from it. Once a sport like triathlon stops being fun, it becomes tedious and failure is a certainty. Always be on the lookout for ways to make your training fun and varied, and the rest will follow. You can do this by taking advantage of your proficiency in three different sports by competing in road running races, bicycle races and mastering swim galas.

Confidence carries you

One of the byproducts of good training is an increased confidence in your ability. But even good preparation isn't always a deterrent to pre-event nerves. The key is to trust your training programme and get to the start line eager to test that training. Every athlete who has ever stood at the starting zone will probably confess to a little self-doubt; the difference between those who succeed and those who don't is the manner in which they learn to overcome those vulnerable feelings.

DAVE SCOTT

Triathlon's first celebrity

During triathlon's fledgling years in the early 1980s, Dave Scott of the USA caused the most ripples after romping home to six Hawaii Ironman World Championships between 1980 and 1987. Although missing wins in 1981 and 1985, Scott was invincible during his first Ironman in 1980 and appeared to dominate the event for eight years.

His first introduction to the Ironman was in 1978 when Ironman inventor John Collins told him in Hawaii about his new event. Scott was already there to compete in one of his favourite events – the 2.4-mile (3.9km) Waikiki Rough Water Swim. At first the thought of adding another 112 miles (180km) of cycling and a full marathon seemed to him to be a bit loony – but Scott was an endurance man by nature and finally in 1980 he capitulated. He decided to take on the challenge.

During the six-win reign that followed, Scott redefined the limits of triathlon. He was the complete all-round athlete, with a mental strength that knew no bounds. Challengers came and went but it was only in 1989 – arguably the greatest Ironman race ever – that American Mark Allen eventually got the better of Scott (both Scott and Allen had a problematic race in 1988 and Scott Molina took the title). In 1989, Allen pulled away in the final 2 miles (3km) after a head-to-head battle that lasted throughout the entire race.

Perhaps Dave Scott's most famous achievement was his second place in the 1994 Hawaii Ironman when, at the age of 40, he got to within a few metres of taking the lead from Australian legend Greg Welch. He followed up this remarkable achievement by finishing fifth in the 1996 race.

By his own admission, Scott never had the raw talent that men like Mark Allen possessed, but his work ethic was exemplary, and he was proof that hard work and dedication are secrets to success. Since Scott's heyday, he has been one of triathlon's greatest ambassadors, and he remains a triathlete superhero, presently imparting his knowledge as a motivational speaker, coach and commentator.

'If you set a goal for yourself and are able to achieve it, you have won your race. Your goal can be to come in first, to improve your performance, or just to finish the race – it's up to you.'

— Dave Scott

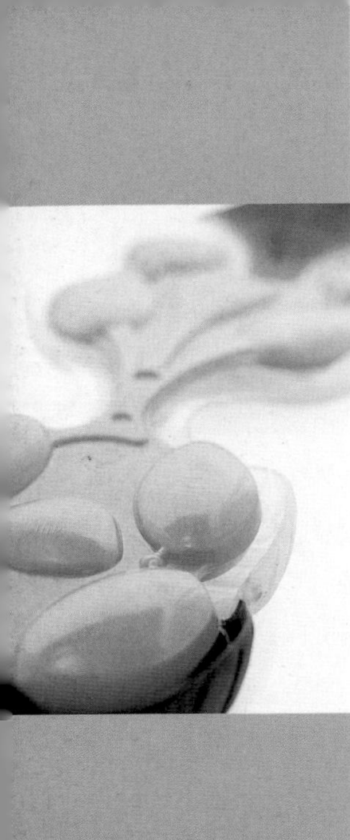

2 GET THE RIGHT GEAR

For triathlon diehards, the next best thing to a long session on a Sunday morning is buying the equipment with which to do it. The good and bad thing about triathlon is that there is so much you can buy. There is no doubt that, more than any other sport, triathlon has all the gadgets, gizmos, accessories, gear and training tools. Great news if you're Bill Gates but bad for your credit rating if you're not. From the basic swimsuit and running vest to the top-of-the-line tri-suits, the average triathlete could spend a small fortune on his sport. It does make sense, though: first you need the swimming gear, then the cycling equipment, and finally that cool running gear. But as if that isn't enough, add the triathlon-specific gear – all-in-one full tri-suits, elastic laces, swimming wetsuits – and you could be looking to extend the mortgage on your home.

The key is knowing what you need to get the maximum enjoyment from your involvement in triathlon.

The basics, however, are still cheap and accessible for even the tightest of budgets. If you're tentatively sticking your toe into the water at your first triathlon, acquiring a Softride beam bike, an Ironman wetsuit and the latest Zoot Hawaii full tri-suit is plain silly. A basic swimsuit, a supermarket mountain bike and a pair of cross trainers is really all you need to take on a Sprint Distance triathlon. I have met many social triathletes who have cheerfully ridden mountain bikes, have never used a wetsuit and who wear their running kit as triathlon gear. And then there are those who simply have a passion for the equipment that triathlon offers and will buy anything they can lay their hands on.

If you enjoy your first triathlon (and I bet you will), purchase your upgrades wisely without being drawn into buying gadgets and gizmos that cost a lot but hardly have any real effect on performance.

In this chapter, you get to decide in which category you belong as a triathlete.

3

SWIMMING

Although a swimsuit is enough to get you through your first triathlon, there are many accessories that will help you specifically in training. Starting with the basics:

Swimsuit

Buy the best quality suit you can afford – you don't want to be walking around with 'saggy butt syndrome' after a couple of months, caused by a poor quality suit losing its shape. Buy one that's a size or more smaller than what is a good fit. When you're in the water, you want to be as streamlined as possible and a tight-fitting swimsuit will perform better. Next time you watch a swimming event on TV, notice how skimpy the apparel is. If you need further proof of the value of a tight fit, try swimming with a pair of baggy shorts on and see how much drag they create.

Also look for a chlorine-resistant suit that will not fade after only a few months.

The tri-suit

Swimsuits are fine for training, but when it comes to taking part in a triathlon, you may want to consider a specialized triathlon outfit. If you're only doing a Sprint Distance event, though, don't splurge out on triathlon-specific gear; only consider doing this for any race from Olympic Distance upward.

Triathlon suits are generally made with stronger seams that can withstand the rigours of cycling and running. Most include a small chamois (padding in the crotch and groin area) similar to that found in cycling shorts. It's worth it if you're going to be on the bike for more than an hour. For a more streamlined swim, the tri-suit needs to be a tight fit. This will also limit unwanted creases that can cause chafing during the running leg.

Goggles

If you don't want the suffering-from-a-hangover bloodshot-eyes look all day, a pair of swimming goggles is essential. It is important to get yourself a good pair – cheap goggles leak, fog up and are uncomfortable. If you're just starting your triathlon career, this will negatively impact on your swimming experience.

Goggles are made in a variety of shapes and sizes. Some come in a narrow fit, sealing into the eye socket, while others come in a wider fit that seals around the eye socket. Select goggles with a silicone seal that moulds to the shape of your face after a while. Foam seals tend to harden and break off, resulting in leaks. When buying your goggles, fit them onto your eyes without taking the straps around the back of your head. If they seal properly, sticking for a few seconds, they fit well. If you can't get a proper seal, then try another pair.

Goggle tip

A full swim mask, made by companies like Seal Mask, is a slimmed-down version of a diving mask and provides a far more comfortable fit around the outside of the eye socket as well as excellent visibility for open-water swims.

Wetsuits

Swimming wetsuits serve two important purposes: they insulate and keep the body warm during cold-water swims (essential for performance and to ward against hypothermia) and they provide buoyancy and speed for both the novice and the professional. Modern wetsuits are so advanced that a top-of-the range specialized triathlon wetsuit can improve swim times by 30% or more.

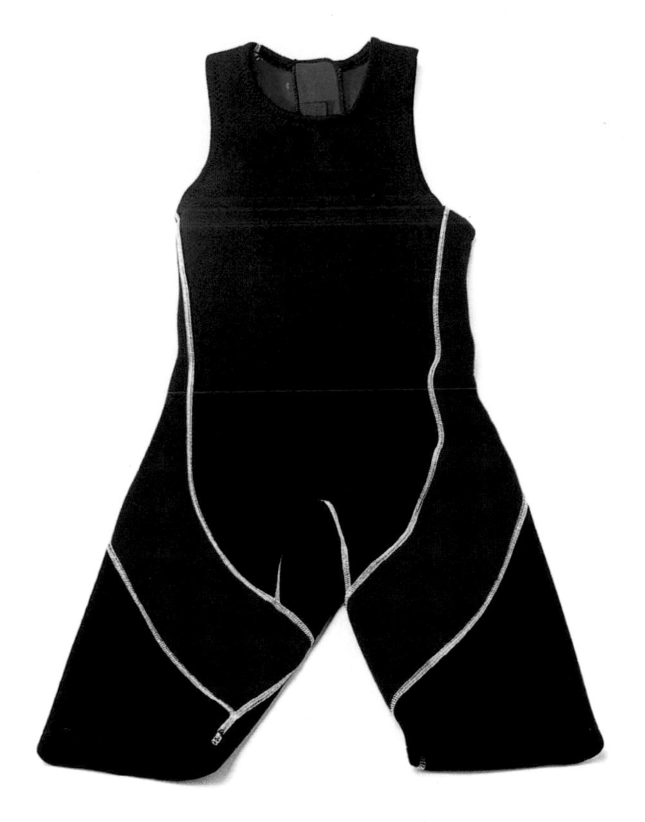

Styles

Although full-cut wetsuits are still the most effective means of maintaining insulation, buoyancy and improving efficiency in the water, they are more restrictive and difficult to peel off. Sleeveless and short-cut suits are now also widely used. Sleeveless wetsuits are preferred by triathletes who need to give their arms more freedom to move during the swim, and short-cut suits are good for faster transition times.

Materials

Most wetsuits are made from neoprene, a soft insulating and pliable rubber that is moulded and layered to be thicker on the body and legs, and thinner on the arms and shoulders. According to Olympic rules, wetsuits are not allowed to be more than 3mm thick although many social triathletes often use dive and surf suits for less important events. International brand names such as Orca, Ironman, Quintana Roo and Aquaman have made a science out of triathlon wetsuits and, though costly, a top end 'wettie' can make a great difference to your in-water performance.

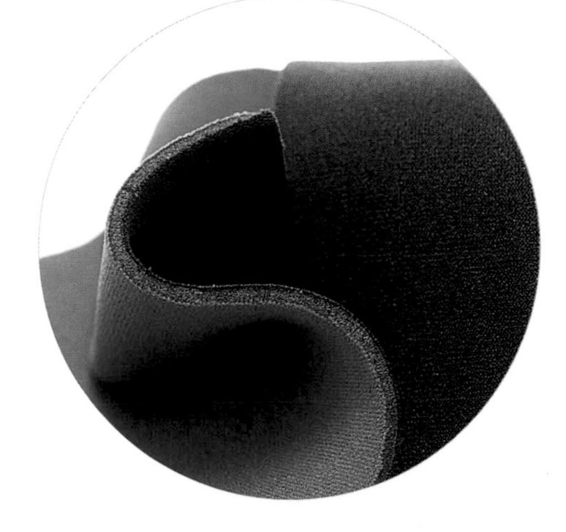

How tight is tight?

The first time you squeeze into a decent swimming wetsuit you'll think you've turned into the Michelin Man. It happened to me. Although I gave my specific measurements to the manufacturer, I found myself almost suffocating from the tight fit and phoned them back to complain that they'd sent me the wrong suit. Only to be told that it would all be okay once I got into the water – and they were right. Once I plunged in, the wetsuit loosened up and the tight fit meant that I swam my best swim split ever. For more on getting in and out of your wetsuit, see Chapter 6, Race Day.

Swimming aids

Once you start to get a little more serious, you will need to invest in a few training extras that are beyond the basics.

Pull buoy

A flotation device, made from polystyrene or buoyant rubber, which is held between the thighs during the swim to keep the lower trunk horizontal in the water. An absolute must when you want to rest weary legs or concentrate on a specific arm technique.

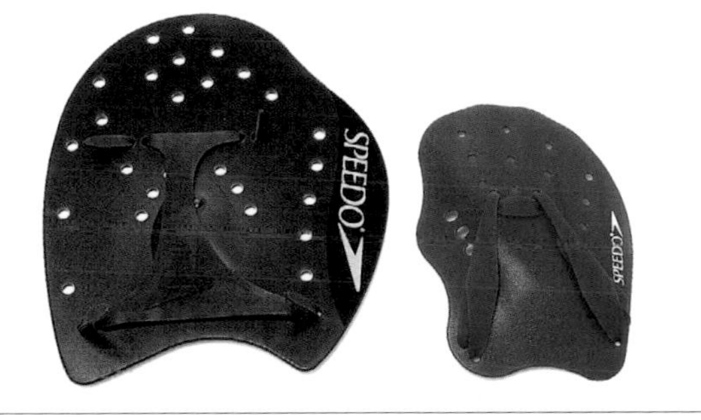

Paddles

These come in a variety of sizes, from large ones to build endurance strength to finger paddles that help with technique. The bigger the paddle, the more the chance of a shoulder injury, so use them sparingly.

Flippers (fins)

These come in both long and short lengths. Short flippers can either be bought or you can simply cut off the ends of a pair of long flippers. They help with kicking-specific drills in the pool or to give an added boost in training during butterfly and backstroke sessions.

Swimcaps

Most indoor pools require the use of a swimcap for hygienic reasons, but a top-quality swimcap certainly can aid your swim. Caps come in silicone (top-end quality), cheap rubber or more comfortable nylon skullcaps.

My choice

When it comes to swimcaps, I prefer the nylon skullcaps because they are simply more comfortable and you don't feel as if your head is in a giant vice after 20 minutes of swimming. Silicone and rubber caps often squeeze your head so tightly that you tend to get a headache after a long session. I use a silicone cap only in races, where being slippery in the water is more important than comfort.

CYCLING

This is where you become the big spender. In starting off, a bottom-end mountain bike and an approved helmet is all you will need to compete, but on becoming more competitive, a little more expense will be necessary. The key to buying good cycling equipment is to ensure that you always feel comfortable. If there is nothing else you remember from this section, make it comfort. Proportionately, you will spend the most number of hours on your bicycle and any discomfort is magnified as time progresses. You can spend thousands on bits and bobs for a bicycle, but if you're not comfortable, the money is wasted.

Bike fit

The key to being comfortable on your bike is to get the correct frame size; and the best way to do that is to buy your bike from a reputable cycle shop. But remember to tell them that you intend to compete in triathlons and use aero (aerodynamic) bars, as this will affect the setup. An effective aerodynamic position in the tri-bars – a flat back, with elbows at 90 degrees while you're resting in the tri-bars – can be achieved on a road bike by modifying the seat position to rotate the rider forward.

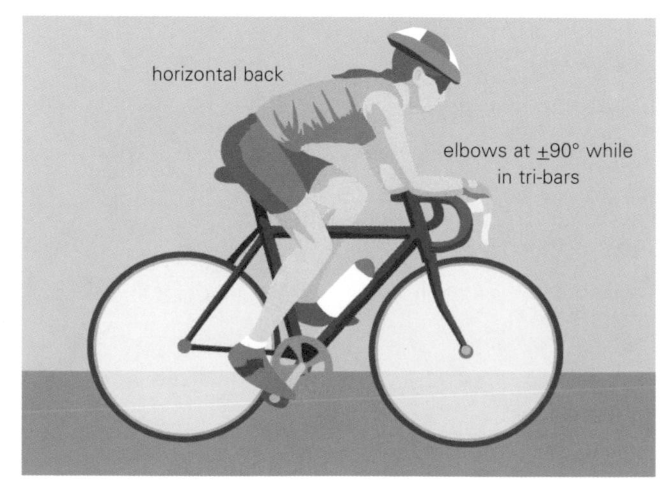

Frame types

From the solid, shock-absorbing and cheaper steel frames to the titanium and carbon-fibre options, present day bicycles are wonders of engineering brilliance.

Steel frames

Usually the cheaper option, steel frames are relatively heavy but solid, and absorb heaps of road rattle. They are reliable workhorses that can do the job just as well in a competitive environment. They generally don't have aerodynamic design features. Steel frames are good for training but a lighter frame is better for racing.

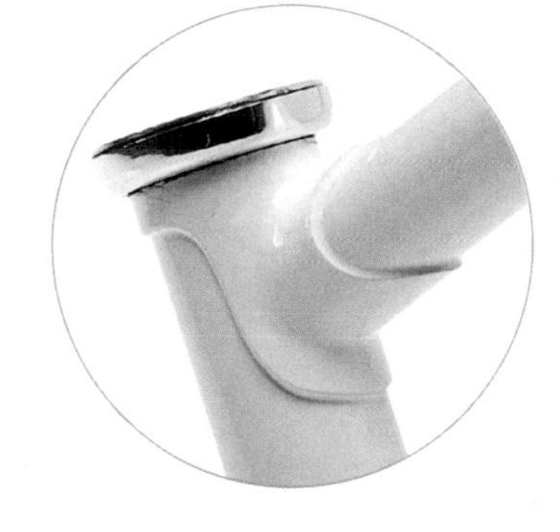

Aluminium

This is far stiffer than steel but it's what makes the bicycle highly responsive (what you put in is what you get out), it's much lighter and relatively cost effective. Due to the unforgiving nature of the frame, though, it tends to lead to more road fatigue. Features aerodynamic designs.

Carbon fibre

Full carbon-fibre-frame bikes are increasingly being manufactured though many triathlon bikes are already fitted with carbon-fibre components (e.g. carbon-fibre forks and pedals). This material is relatively stiff, light and does a good job absorbing road shock. First generation carbon-fibre bikes often cracked at stress points but modern-day examples are reliable and effective. Aerodynamic designs available.

Titanium

The *crème de la crème* of bicycle frames, titanium is a superlight, superstrong alloy that adequately absorbs road shock – but the frame stiffness and lightness make titanium frames expensive. Features aero designs.

Tri-bike vs road bike

Competing in the cycling leg of a triathlon is known as time trialling – getting from the cycle start to the cycle finish in the fastest time possible. As a result, many cycle companies like Corima, Softride, Zipp and Quintana Roo have developed specialized triathlon bikes with two principles in mind: aerodynamics and maximizing power. Hence the arrival of aero frames instead of round-tube frames and specialized deep-section wheels (see right). Unfortunately for the triathlon-age groupie, specialized aero frames make very little difference to performance since you need to be travelling at over 30kph (19mph) to get any benefit from it. Ironically, many top pros don't even bother with these specialized frames simply for the reason that the differences are marginal. At the end of the day, it's the rider's legs that make the biggest difference.

One of the most effective aerodynamic innovations is the seat-tube angle. Normal road bikes have a seat-tube angle of 72 degrees to allow full use of all the leg muscles and optimize efficiency over all types of terrain. Developers later discovered that a more upright angle of 76–78 degrees allowed for a more aerobody position while also putting less strain on the quadricep muscles, which are used for the final running leg. On a relatively flat course, this steeper angle was ideal although performance on climbs was somewhat reduced.

Some manufacturers like Cannondale also developed smaller, lighter 650c wheels as opposed to the traditional 700c wheels, to reduce rolling resistance, offsetting the effects of the new sitting position on hills. (The 'c' does not denote any metric or imperial measurement; it is a means of indicating a specific size.)

When choosing your bike, the most important aspect is to look closely at your ability, the kind of terrain you are likely to train and race on and effective use of funds.

GETTING THE MOST FROM YOUR BIKE

Small changes in equipment can mean big changes in performance without having to sell off your children. The table below indicates how to transform an ordinary bike into a competitive machine.

Percentage time savings established in a study carried out at the University of Texas, TX, USA.

Frame

An entry-level frame with midrange equipment, standard wheels and standard pedals.

You can add:

Gizmos

Streamlined water bottles, aero seat tubes and aero helmets all help to make the rider and his bike more slippery through the air, but these should be last on your list of priorities.

How to choose a bike

1. Comfort
2. Comfort
3. Aero position and comfort
4. Tri-bars, aero wheels
5. Lightness, frame composition and equipment

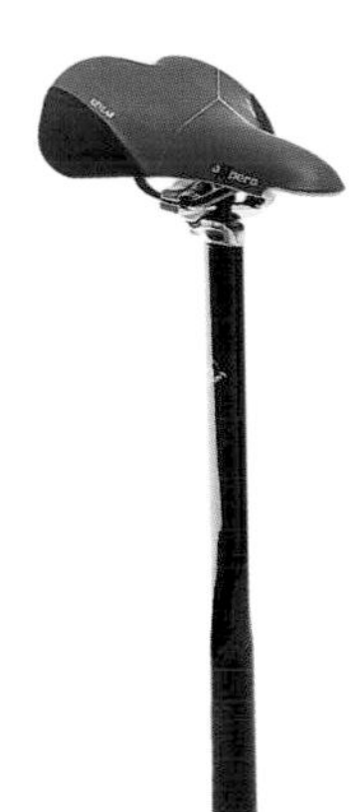

Seat-tube angle

Most bicycles are made for all-round performance, but by changing the angle of the seat tube you can help increase pedalling power in the aero position as your body is more directly over the pedals.

Tri-bars

Depending on your level of ability to hold the aero position, you can improve your bike times by as much as *15%. The flatter your profile the faster you'll go!

Clipless pedals

If there's one item of equipment every bike rider should have, it's clipless pedals. Yes, straps are better than standard factory pedals but clipless pedals into which stiff, cycling-specific shoes are hooked (these promote better energy transfer to the pedals) make a huge difference in generating power. Bike times can be improved by at least *30%.

Aero wheels

Good quality hubs and deep-section rims can improve times by another *5–10% depending on the terrain. When buying rims think good quality hubs first and follow with aero rims – which only really benefit the rider at speeds over 30kph (19mph). Air resistance can be further reduced by using disc wheels, the more versatile deep-section rims, and by looking at the number and design of the spokes.

Cycling shoes

Ideally the triathlete should have two pairs of cycling shoes. One pair is designed specifically for training, with multi-straps that help to keep the foot in place. Then, because of transitions it's important also to have a pair of shoes that is easy to get in and out of. You can either buy triathlon-specific shoes like those made by Carnac, which feature a single wide Velcro strap across the top of the foot, making it easy to tighten; or you can adapt normal cycling shoes, e.g., by trimming off the centre strap on a three-strap shoe and taking out the centre tongue.

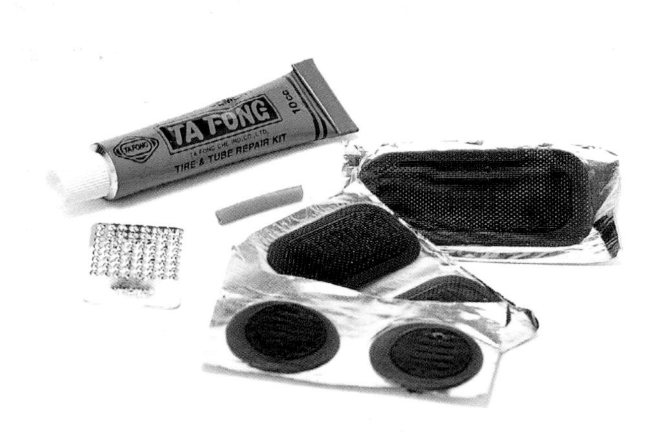

Repair equipment

It sounds obvious, but always remember to take a puncture repair kit, pump and a set of Allen keys whenever you're out training. If you've ever had the misfortune to experience Murphy's Law, you will know that punctures, loose bike stems or minor technical problems only occur when you don't have the means to fix them.

Tyres

Good quality high-pressure clincher-type tyres (right) are still the best buy. Both modern clincher tyres and tubeless 'tubbies' can be pumped up relatively hard, but clinchers cost far less. Clinchers comprise an outer rubber tyre with an inner tube; the pressure of the inflated tube holds the outer tyre in a U-shaped wheel rim, i.e. it 'clinches' the rim. Tubbies are complete tyres that are stuck on the rim.

Helmet

Never skimp on buying a good-quality helmet that fits correctly and is comfortable. (Yes, most of the Tour de France competitors may well have cycled without helmets in the past, but notice that one of the greatest – Lance Armstrong – never fails to wear one).

Check your fit by placing the helmet on top of your head without buckling the chin strap, then tilt your head from side to side. There should be very little movement of the helmet and the fit should be snug but not tight.

If you ever crash, hitting your helmet in the process, *always* replace the helmet. It will often show only superficial damage, but internally the polystyrene may have been crushed and compacted, and it therefore will lose its protective qualities.

Eyewear

Buying eyewear – whether lenses are specifically clear or tinted against sun glare – is a personal choice, but highly recommended. When travelling at high speed, your eyes are subjected to hurricane-like wind, while the phenomenon of 'wind burn' (when you get sunburnt on a windy day) seriously affects the health of your eyes. Glasses also protect against flying stones, insects and dust.

When buying eyewear for training, look for frames that are comfortable, light and fit snugly around the eyes (so they don't bounce), and that won't shatter in the event of an accident. Never buy glass lenses; many high-end sunglasses have lenses that easily pop out in an accident. Make your choice wisely and buy quality if at all possible.

Cycling tip

Buying a good-quality second-hand bicycle can often be better than a cheaper 'new' bike, but remember that comfort and fit are primary factors, and make sure that the quality of the frame and components is good.

RUNNING

Establishing your foot type

All feet undergo a certain action during running. As the foot hits the ground, it strikes at the back of the heel and then rolls forward and in (this is called pronation), before the 'toe-off' power phase. Most runners will have a different rate of pronation, and this needs to be taken into account when selecting a shoe. To establish your foot type, do the wet foot test: stand in water and then on a dry area of the ground where you can clearly see your footprint (see illustration). When you consult a good shoe store (this is essential!), there are four distinct shoe categories.

Neutral/cushioning

For runners with neutral biomechanics, these shoes have little in the way of anti-pronation technology but are usually well cushioned. Also suitable for supinators (see illustration), who possess less shock-absorbing ability than pronators; a neutral shoe with a semi- curved last and good forefoot and rear foot cushioning is recommended.

Anti-pronation

Excessive pronators are biomechanically less efficient. They need motion control shoes with straight lasts (the shape of the underside of the sole) so anti-pronation shoes usually include heel counters and sole stabilizers to slow the rate of pronation and thereby prevent injury to the lower leg. Mild pronators can handle stability shoes which are designed with a semi-curved last.

Motion control

For runners suffering from severe biomechanical difficulties and also needing pronation control. These shoes are straight-lasted, extremely stable, and heavy.

Racers

Minimalist in design, racers are light, neutral and flexible to aid toe-off. These shoes are made specifically for racing. A curved last limits the supportive areas to the forefoot and outer heel, allowing more flexibility elsewhere. Ideal for short-distance races, if they *are* used over longer distances they are suitable only for the elite athletes.

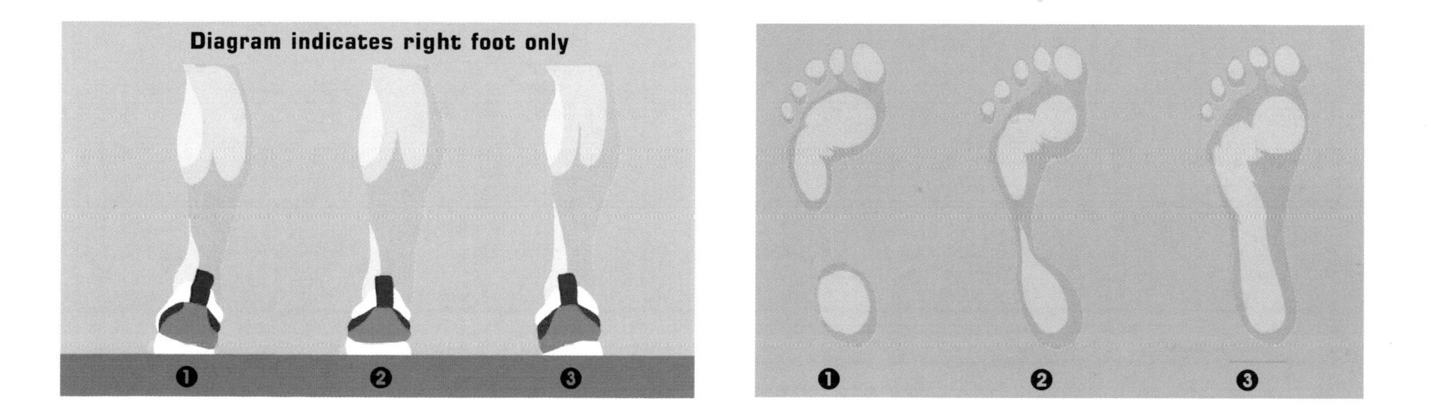

1. SUPINATOR
Foot doesn't roll over before toe-off, but rolls to the side.

2. NEUTRAL
Ideal biomechanics. No overpronation.

3. OVERPRONATOR
Foot rolls in excessively during the foot strike.

3 SWIM, CYCLE, RUN

As already mentioned in this book, the sport of triathlon has the advantage over many other sports in that boredom is rarely a factor. Even mediocre triathletes can participate in swimming galas, then mix with the cyclists in a road race and also compete in road running with a great deal of success. What a bonus! This truly dynamic sport allows you to become a tradesman in three different fields.

The downside is that to be proficient in three sports requires time spent practising and specifically training in three different ways. The challenge to find the time and the physical and mental commitment are unrivalled in other sports. Top-class triathletes can train up to six hours a day while even amateur triathletes who are attempting a race like an Ironman will be required to put in at least three to four hours of training a day during peak training periods.

Throughout this chapter, the main focus is on technique for all three triathlon disciplines. Since, for the most part, the people reading this book are unlikely to be professional athletes, time management is key to maximizing potential. Which is why technique is important. By focusing on the most energy-efficient way of swimming, cycling and running, you get to spend less time training but you still get the same benefit. Therefore, you need to maintain a constant awareness of your form.

If technique fails you during a session, it is better to stop, refocus, then concentrate on your activity. Simply training without focusing on how you train gives you no benefit and may even harm the way in which you will race.

The same applies to maximizing the time you can spend training. Having specific goals, preplanning your training and varying your workouts will help make every session count.

It all sounds rather intimidating – training goals, planned training sessions and goal races. And it is. That's why you need to be reminded of the importance of keeping your training fun. Revel in the variety offered by the three sports, the joy of being able to compete in three disciplines – and continue to challenge yourself.

MAKING THE MOST OF YOUR TRAINING

The key to training for triathlon is to give every session a purpose and a short-term goal, all leading to a long-term goal. So plan ahead to ensure that every session counts. In all three disciplines there are three distinct areas of training that need to be included in a weekly training programme. This chapter will focus on four elements within each discipline.

Technique work

Probably most vital in swimming, working on technique will produce far more rewards than flat-out training. Technique work involves isolating various elements of your physical action to modify them through practice and thereby condition the body to work efficiently.

Aerobic training

The foundation of any training programme, this takes the form of longer but easier sessions at a moderate heart-rate pace. Building cardiovascular fitness and forming the building blocks for speed and strength training, it involves longer periods of training at a low intensity.

Strength and speedwork

Strength work (from gym work to cycling uphill in a hard gear with slow leg turnover) builds muscle, strengthens ligaments and tendons, and teaches mental resilience. Speedwork focuses on challenging the body to move faster through short intervals followed by long rest periods.

Recovery

This can take the form of active recovery i.e. playing a game of tennis, or complete recovery where the athlete takes a day off. The body and the mind need at least one day off a week from any training whatsoever. For beginners, two days of complete rest every week is advisable.

RESISTANCE (GYM) TRAINING

In your gym routine, follow a base or building phase (muscle- and strength endurance), a competition programme and a recovery phase to maximize the benefits and allow the body to adequately adapt.

Muscle endurance phase

(2–6 weeks)

Focus: circuit-training and general body conditioning.

▶ Select 12–15 exercises from the gym circuit; 2–3 sets per core exercise; 12–20 repetitions in a minute per set; rest 30–60 seconds between sets; 2–3 sessions a week.

Strength-endurance phase

(4–6 weeks)

Focus: more specific triathlon conditioning.

▶ Select 8–10 exercises; 4–6 sets per core exercise; 8–12 repetitions per minute per set; rest periods 1–2 minutes between sets; 2–4 sessions a week.

Strength and power phase

(4–8 weeks)

Focus: exercises set out in this section.

▶ 7 exercises; 3–5 sets per core exercise; 6–8 repetitions per minute per set; 2–3 minutes rest between sets; 2–4 sessions per week.

Competition phase

Focus: specific conditioning, targeting weak areas while focusing on core exercises. Fit in resistance training around competitions.

▶ 1–2 sets per exercise; 6–15 repetitions per minute per set; 1–2 sessions a week.

Active recovery phase

(4–8 weeks)

Focus: non-specific training that is unrelated to triathlon to allow for recovery.

SUGGESTED ROUTINE

BENCH PRESS 1

Muscles: Pectoralis major, anterior deltoid, triceps

❶ Lying on a bench, feet shoulder-width apart on the floor, hold weights (overhand grip) at each side of the chest. Extend arms, pushing dumbbells above chest till they touch, palms facing forward.

❷ Slowly lower dumbbells to the chest, then push up to starting position.

❶ ❷

2 CHIN-UP

Muscles: Latissimus dorsi, trapezius (upper) biceps, brachialis

❶ **Note:** hands should hold chin-up bar with a *narrower* (overhand) grip than that shown here. Hang with arms extended (hands placed shoulder-width apart) and knees flexed.

❷ Pull body up vertically till chin is raised above the bar. Hold briefly, then return slowly to extended arm position.

❶

❷

3 KNEE TUCK

Muscles: Rectus abdominus, hip flexors

❶ Lying flat on the floor, legs extended, arms at your sides, lift head and curl upper back and shoulders off the floor.

❷ Raise upper torso, simultaneously pulling knees towards the chest while hands move forward alongside legs. Hold, then extend slowly till upper back and legs are slightly raised off the floor.

❶

❷

4 INCLINE LEG PRESS

Muscles: Quadriceps, gluteus maximus

❶ Leaning against backrest with feet on foot platform, placed shoulder-width apart and slightly turned out, hold handles and take weight load on the legs.

❷ Keeping knees slightly bent throughout, flex to just over 90° till thighs and platform are about parallel. Slowly extend legs to push platform to starting position.

STEP-UP

5

Muscles: Quadriceps, gluteus maximus, hamstrings

❶ Face bench, supporting barbell on the shoulders with an overhand grip, hands and feet shoulder-width apart.

❷ Keeping back straight and torso upright, step onto bench with right leg, pushing to lift torso and left leg onto bench. Step down with right foot, following with the left. Alternate leading legs.

PRONE LEG CURL

6

Muscles: Hamstrings

❶ Lie face down on the curl machine, making sure to keep head and upper body flat on the bench throughout. Place ankles under footpads and take hold of the handles.

❷ Use legs to curl in footpad as close to buttocks as possible. Hold briefly, then slowly return to starting position.

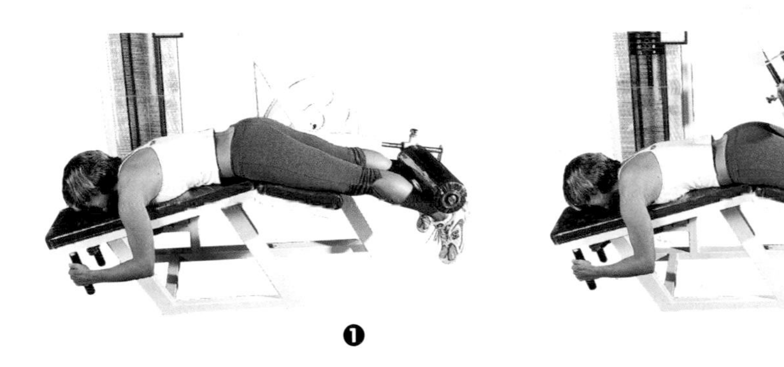

CALF RAISES

7

Muscles: Soleus, gastrocnemius

❶ With pads resting on the shoulders, stand on foot platform with balls of the feet only and take hold of handles to stabilize yourself. Keep toes pointing straight and the knees slightly flexed throughout.

❷ Slowly lower heels as deep as you can, then raise them as high as possible.

SWIMMING TRAINING

Of all the three disciplines, swimming is arguably the one element of triathlon that turns away many potential participants. Not surprising. Once you've seen the mass of flailing hands and arms at the start of a triathlon it can be rather intimidating for anyone who hasn't undergone a 'life-savers' hell' week. To the uninitiated, swimming looks simply dangerous. Stories of frigid water, kicks in the face and black eyes are hardly a good advertisement.

Then again, ask any experienced triathlete what part of the triathlon he or she least worries about, it will most probably be the swimming section. The reasons are simple:

For one, compared to the length of the other two disciplines, swimming will almost certainly be the shortest part of the triathlon – not only in distance but also in time.

Secondly, you go into the swim section when you're at your freshest, and with logic and a little tactical savvy there are ways and means to niftily avoid the nasty repercussions of being in a limb-infested washing machine (see Chapter 6, Race Day, for more tactics for the open-water swim).

The mechanics of swimming

Any top swimming coach will tell you that correct technique, body position and efficiency are far more valuable to the swimmer than brute strength and powerful muscles. In a study done at the 1996 Olympic Games, a team of swimming specialists counted the number of strokes that each of the finalists took across the length of the pool. Almost always, the swimmers who took the least number of strokes finished best, proving that to be efficient, less strokes are needed.

If you get to see giant Australian Ian Thorpe in action, watch how slowly his arm turnover is; he looks as if he's out for a gentle swim with mates. Belying it all is a perfect streamlined body position and a powerful but efficient technique under and above the water.

Bilateral blowout

One of my coach's favourite drills was a session where you would breathe only every third stroke on alternate sides. Not only does it encourage more balanced swimming, it also builds more lung strength.

Don't be scared

Take it from someone who used to be an absolute non-swimmer: the swimming leg is not that bad. Once you know this, use it as a motivational weapon as you learn to face your fear through preparation and training. When it comes to swimming, confidence is everything – and confidence only comes from doing the lengths in the pool. As a rough guide, you should be able to swim 85% of the race distance with ease. For example, if you're swimming 1500m in a race, you should be able to swim 1200m comfortably.

Join a squad

Swimming alone is a bit like having a party and no one turns up. It's demotivating, demoralizing and lonely. If you're a novice, try to hook up with a squad of social master swimmers who will cater for a wide range of abilities. As you progress, you can join up with a specialized swimming squad and coach to help improve your technique and keep you motivated.

Vary your workouts

If you are forced to do swim workouts on your own, life as a swim triathlete need not be over. The key is to vary the session as much as possible (see swimming drills pp52–53). Simply diving in and swimming 40 lengths across a 25m pool is about as exciting as watching a TV test pattern. Rather break up the session into a 15-length warm-up, throw in 10 x 2-length intervals and finish with a gentle 5-length cool-down. The more you vary your swim workouts, the more exciting they will be.

ABOVE RIGHT *A good swimmer has learnt to master technique first and foremost, and makes strength and fitness secondary.*

Mimic the open water

It's fine to swim like a tuna when you've got a black line on the bottom of the pool to work from, but what happens when below you is a muddy nothingness, the view from your goggles looks like the inside of a washing machine and your sense of direction is nothing but a blurry maze on the horizon? Remember those swim practice drills that force you to take your head out of the water instead of relying on the black line for guidance. You can also mimic race situations during training by doing sets that force you to start out fast, find an early rhythm and finish strongly.

Practise in an easy session

It is not easy to practise something that doesn't come naturally, so use your warm-up phase to practise swimming one length breathing on one side, then the next length breathing on the opposite side. Trying to perfect bilateral breathing while focusing on speed or technique makes the job doubly difficult.

Body position

The ideal body position is as horizontal as possible. The less the legs drag behind the body, the faster the speed. During the 'glide' phase of the stroke, the body needs to be as long as possible. Taller swimmers clearly have an advantage over shorter swimmers, although traditionally the shorter athletes get their own back during the running leg. There are two relatively simple drills that help the swimmer establish the correct body position.

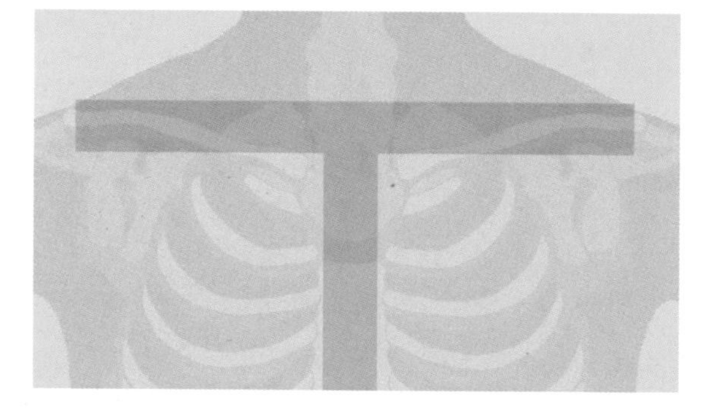

The Magic T

During training, imagine that an iron rod extends in a vertical line from the base of your neck to the end of your coccyx, and that your shoulders are connected across the top of it in the shape of a 'T'.

Head down

Most swimmers keep their head too high in the water. Practise 'pushing' your head down into the water and lifting up your butt – almost as if you're swimming downhill. This exaggerated pose may seem a little weird at first, but the more you practise, the more horizontal your body will be and the more your head will sit in the ideal bow wave created by the water.

Use the pull buoy

Although the pull buoy is designed to help isolate the arms so you can work on specific arm technique, it also helps your body get used to a good horizontal position since its float attributes raise the upper body above the water line. But don't be lazy – the pull buoy only plays a minor role in helping with body position.

Balanced swimming

The best way to cope with an open-water swim is being able to breathe on both sides. Yes, I know, easier said than done. Depending on your preferred side, the other breathing side will always seem a little awkward, but practice – especially in this case – makes perfect. Once you can master the art, it will help balance your stroke, prevent overuse injuries and make you better able to cope with an open-water swim. Try the following drills.

Demonstration of front crawl

The entry

This is the phase of the stroke where the front arm enters the water beyond the head, then extends even further out to help create momentum.

The catch

When the hand starts to bend slightly in the water at the top of the stroke, with the body fully extended on one side to create pulling power.

The pull

Using a sculling S-shaped motion (sculling creates both lift and power as the hand maps out an S-shape from the top of the stroke to the finish), the arm bends at roughly 90 degrees and then pulls back with arm and hand towards the centre of the body.

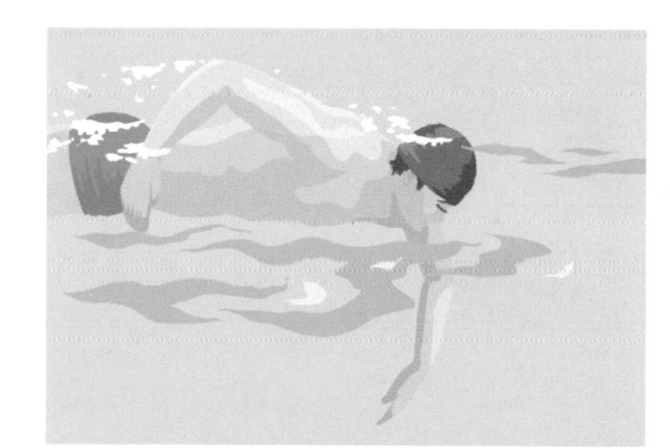

The finish

The final phase of the stroke where the hand pushes back under the water and straightens before leaving the water for the recovery

DRILLS TO IMPROVE TECHNIQUE

It needs to be said again: technique in swimming is everything. I've seen spindly 14-year-old schoolgirls drill the Speedos off the testosterone-charged musclemen in the gym pool simply because they had superior technique. Study carefully the demonstration on the Front Crawl (see p49), then try at least two of the following drills every time you get into the pool. Do these drills preferably with a pull buoy, except for the drill involving legs only, so you can concentrate on your arms.

Catch-up

This is a classic. During the entry phase of the crawl stroke when the hand enters the water at the top of the stroke, keep one arm extended in front of you, but only start the catch and pull phase once you've brought the alternate arm over and parallel to the extended arm. For a brief moment both arms will be straight above you. This helps slow the stroke down.

Fisting

Instead of swimming with an open hand, keep your hands clenched in a fist. Because there's little power being exerted by the hand, you will naturally depend more on using your entire arm to create pull.

One-armed drills

By swimming alternate lengths using one arm only – the opposite arm is stretched out above the head – this allows you to focus on that particular arm's pulling action. Concentrate on pulling long and using a sculling action throughout the power phase of the stroke.

High elbow

The higher your elbow is in recovery, the less stress you put on your shoulder muscles during swimming and the more efficient you will be. There are many variations to the theme, but try this drill to improve your high elbow recovery: during the recovery phase of your stroke, make sure your thumb touches your ear on its way through to the catch phase of the stroke. It will exaggerate the action, but will help get your arm used to a high elbow recovery. Do five lengths either side.

Legs only

In long-distance swimming, kicking is less important than in sprint events, but that doesn't mean you should neglect your kicking. An excellent exercise is to hold a kicker board out in front of you and do four to six lengths of pure kicking every session. Concentrate on fast, short kicks, making an effort to keep ankles and feet relaxed.

Sight-breathing

To perfect your ability to lift your head (not your shoulders) out of the water to see where you're going in a race while breathing at the same time (known as sight-breathing), do a set where you lift your head and look forward every fourth or fifth stroke in the pool to breathe. You can alternate lengths of normal crawl breathing, i.e. taking your head to the side, with lengths of sight-breathing crawl.

Swimming paddles

These come in two types: big paddles and finger paddles. Big paddles cover the entire hand and should only be used during long intervals. Doing sprints with big paddles puts extra pressure on the shoulders and could cause injury. Finger paddles are smaller, only fitting across the hand's fingers. You can use these paddles to help perfect your hand position during the recovery and catch phase of the stroke.

Long and slow

At least once a week do one session of long-distance slow swimming. It doesn't only help to build your aerobic capacity but also helps to develop good technique.

PUTTING THE DRILLS INTO PRACTICE

Below are some examples of sessions (based on a 25m pool) to help you make the most of this technique in training using speed, endurance and open-water swimming. Obviously the distances will vary according to your proposed race distance, but the principles remain the same.

Beginner sessions for novices

Example 1:

Warm-up:	100m crawl/breaststroke
Drills:	Do 2 lengths of 3 drills
Main set:	5 x 50m (2 lengths)
Endurance:	Swim continuously for 5 min. – easy
Cool-down:	300m crawl/breaststroke

Example 2:

Warm-up:	300m crawl/breaststroke including drills
Drills:	Do 2 lengths of 3 drills
Main set:	3 x 100m (4 lengths) with full recovery
Endurance:	20 lengths alt. crawl and breaststroke
Cool-down:	200m alt. crawl and easy breaststroke

(To build your own programme, add your 10% increase in effort to the programme every second week.)

Endurance

Example 1:

Warm-up:	Easy 500m (20 lengths)
Main set:	(Pyramids)
	50m (2 lengths) on 1 min.
	100m (4 lengths) on 2 min.
	200m (8 lengths) on 4:30 min.
	100m on 2 min.
	50m on 1 min.
	200m on 4:30 min.
	(Repeat all of the above three times)
Cool-down:	Easy 500m alternating freestyle and breaststroke for every lap

Example 2:

Warm-up:	Easy 500m including 300m drills
Main set:	2 x 400m with 3-min. rest
	2 x 200m with 2-min. rest
	2 x 100m with 1-min. rest
Cool-down:	Easy 500m

Make sense of the shorthand

During a swimming session: the phrase 'on 1 min.' means that 1 minute is the total time for that interval – including the rest period – before the next interval should be undertaken.

For example:

If the session says: 50m on 1 min., you have 1 minute to do 50m, then recover before the next interval. Aim to finish the 50m *under* 1 minute to give yourself time to recover before the next interval, i.e. if you swim 50m in 45 seconds, you will have 15 seconds to recover for the next set.

Speed sessions

Example 1:

Warm-up:	Easy 200m followed by 300m drills
Main set:	10 x 25m hard on 2 minutes
Cool-down:	Easy 200m

Example 2:

Warm-up:	Easy 200m followed by 200m drills
Main set:	4 x 100m followed by full recovery
Cool-down:	Easy 500m including drills

Advanced sessions

Example 1:

Warm-up:	400m easy crawl
Main set:	10 x 100m on 1:30–1:45 moderate pace
	400m with kicker board
	400m with pull buoy
	8 x 50m on 1 min. at 85% effort
	200m easy
	8 x 25m sprint at maximum effort
Cool-down:	400m alternating crawl, backstroke, breaststroke

Example 2:

Warm-up:	Easy 200m
Main set:	8 x 400m on 6–7 min. using race pace as a guide
	4 x 25m sprint
Cool-down:	Easy 200m

OPEN-WATER SWIMMING

It often comes as a shock when swimmers are forced to swim in an open-water environment with hundreds of equally nervous competitors. Here are some tips to make it a breeze.

Swim in a squad

Squad training is an excellent way of getting used to the turbulence caused by other swimmers.

Practise sight-breathing

Sight-breathing will then come more naturally when you need to find your bearings in the sea or lake.

Swim outdoors

Organize to swim in open water every couple of weeks with a group of training partners – and a back-up boat just in case you get into trouble.

Start slowly

Don't charge off too quickly – you'll get into oxygen debt.

Start on the fringes

If you're not a strong swimmer, start an open-water swim on the outer flanks of the race, furthest away from the first turning buoy. Avoid being on the inside lane.

Follow those feet

Yes, slipstream. The swimmer in front provides a 30% saving in energy by breaking the water in front, and can also be your eyes, doing the sighting for you.

Warm-up

Do a few drills and sprints to get the body used to the water temperature, especially for a 'dry' land start. Charging into cold water can leave you breathless and panicky.

BIKE TRAINING

If you want to know how to be a good bike rider, beg for or borrow the videotapes of the most recent Tour de France races and watch Lance Armstrong over and over again. The perfect example of the ultimate cyclist, this five-time Tour de France champion started off his cycling career as a triathlete himself. We can learn the following from Armstrong:

Cadence

Watch the speed at which Armstrong pedals (i.e. his cadence). Over a time trial, Armstrong will hold a cadence of over 100. Learning to cycle at a high cadence is one of the fundamental skills of being a good bike rider – you are more efficient, as you rely on longer-lasting aerobic strength ahead of brute force. You should aim for a cadence of between 80 and 90rpm – or if you can, up to 100rpm.

Work this out by counting your number of pedal strokes over 15 seconds, then multiply by four. Don't stress – you'll soon get to learn what a good cadence is without having to continually count. Cadence is all about rhythm, so start off any cycle leg or training session in a light gear and good cadence, then increase the size of the gear once your rhythm has hit the groove.

Full power

In one of Armstrong's scientific lab tests, he discovered that instead of pedalling in circles, he was pedalling simply by pushing down and pulling up. Learn to transfer power throughout the entire pedal stroke by imagining that you're trying to clean a little dog poop off your shoe. That action of dragging your foot along the ground forcefully is exactly the action you need to imitate in your pedalling stroke.

Comfort

Through careful refinements, Armstrong's entire body position is designed around comfort and efficiency. In time trials, Armstrong's back is parallel to his top tube, his knees are close to the centre of the bike and his body position is relaxed and comfortable (see pp28–31). Never sacrifice comfort for speed, however. If you're uncomfortable on the bike, you'll be inefficient anyway.

Saddle height

During time trials, Armstrong slightly raises his saddle height to better incorporate the use of his quadricep muscles. However, your legs should never be fully extended at the bottom end of the power stroke.

Saddle position

Since time trialling is normally about flat-out speed, concentrate on being as far forward on the saddle as possible. This helps you generate better power and saves your hamstrings for the run. You can improve this forward position by investing in an angled seat post or a specialist time trial bike, but it's still possible to adjust a normal road bike by moving the seat forward and concentrating on sitting on the front 'nose' of the saddle.

Aero bars

All modern time trial bikes have aero, or tri, bars. The bars should be positioned parallel to the ground, which allows the rider to keep low and aerodynamic – Armstrong's position is perfect.

Focus

To go fast, you need to concentrate. The best time triallists look just ahead of them and glance up only once in a while to check the road in front of them. By concentrating on a point just ahead, you can focus on keeping a good, still, upper-body position, relaxing your shoulders (an upper body that's not tense helps conserve energy) and concentrating on maintaining your pedal speed without worrying about what your competitors are doing around you. For elites riding in a group in draft-legal races, that focus is more intense. In a group situation, concentration is paramount as the smallest mistake can ruin not only your race but also the race and physical safety of your fellow competitors.

Cut the corners

Concentrate on finding the shortest route. Ride on the inside of bends and corners, but only if it's safe during the race. The same applies to the run leg

Pace judgement

In every race, there are plenty of triathletes who start like Lance Armstrong but end up finishing like a half-dead tortoise. Remember that the cycle leg is only the middle leg of the triathlon – you still have to run! The key to a good cycle leg is to concentrate on maintaining a good cadence and finishing faster than you started. This is where Armstrong differs, however. As he only does the cycle leg, he can afford to go as hard as possible through his time trial.

The long ride

Typically in a triathlon, the cycle leg takes almost twice as long as the run and three times as long as the swim. Therefore it makes sense to spend at least double your training time on cycling. The key to better biking lies in long, steady rides that focus on form and comfort while building a solid endurance base. You should spend at least twice the time of any other ride during the week on your weekly long ride. Remember to keep the effort level easy.

PAULA NEWBY-FRASER

Supreme ironwoman

Regarded by many as the greatest triathlete of them all, former South African Newby-Fraser has won over 20 Ironman titles worldwide, including eight titles at the World Championships in Hawaii. If there is anyone who can claim to be bigger than the sport, it is this 'Ironwoman'.

After the 1988 Hawaii Ironman where she finished 11th, ABC's Wide World of Sports celebrated her as 'the greatest all-round female athlete in the world'. She was also listed in *Sports Illustrated* magazine as among the 60 greatest female athletes of the last century and *Triathlete* magazine rightly named her 'the greatest of all time'. A good swimmer, great cyclist and solid runner, Newby-Fraser simply put all three disciplines together better than any woman.

In 1997, in a poll conducted by CNN and the newspaper *USA Today*, she was listed together with tennis players Martina Navratilova, Steffi Graf, Chris Evert and Billie Jean King as being among the top five professional female athletes over the preceding 25 years. During her 10-year dominance of the Hawaii Ironman World Championships between 1986 and 1996, Newby-Fraser became an icon for women in sport, proving that members of the fairer sex were capable of taking on such an event. With her good looks, muscular frame and trend-setting style, she was more than just a world-class athlete – rather a walking advertisement for all that is inspirational about triathlon.

She continues to compete in Ironman events across the globe. Her 1994 world record of 08:50:53 at Ironman Germany remains unbeaten. In 2001, at age 39, she finished fourth at the Hawaii Ironman. At the close of 2002, 'PNF' (as she is fondly referred to by the triathlon community) had secured 23 Ironman wins worldwide. Compare that with the wins achieved by both Mark Allen and fellow female pioneer Erin Baker (New Zealand), who each won eight, and Dave Scott, who won seven.

Although still competing in selected events near her present home in San Diego, the 'world's greatest-ever triathlete' now imparts her knowledge as a coach on the website multisports.com – good news for the rest of us!

'Everyone has limits on the time they can devote to exercise, and cross training simply gives you the best return on your investment: balanced fitness with minimum injury risk and maximum fun.'

— Paula Newby-Fraser

CYCLING SESSIONS

Try out a method used by top Russian duathletes. Set up your bike on a stationary trainer. In a moderate gear at a moderate effort level, close your eyes and focus on how your muscles work: the pedalling action; the way you sit on the bike; the position of your head and body. Aim for efficient, relaxed pedalling and a relaxed, comfortable upper body position.

Improve your technique

Try this simple drill when you're out on an easy ride. After a good warm-up, concentrate on only using one leg for 1 minute before alternating with the other leg. You can even remove one leg from the pedal. By using a single leg, you're forced to transfer power throughout the pedal stroke. Working out on an indoor trainer, and particularly on a set of rollers (if you dare!), is an ideal way to improve technique, since your concentration is focused purely on your form and not on what's happening on the road.

Strength

There are plenty of drills you can do by alternating the size of your gear, but the easiest way to gain strength is to ride an undulating course in just one gear. Top cyclists often train with a fixed gear and wheel similar to those used by track cyclists. You can simulate this on a normal bike by selecting a midrange gear (such as 38–16) and keeping it there for the duration of the ride. You'll use lots of pure muscle to climb the hills and you'll gain good cadence training by spinning the gear on the downhills.

Build endurance

Once a week, do a cycle at least twice as long as any other cycle of the week; concentrate on an easy aerobic effort level (below 75% of maximum heart rate) while maintaining a high cadence. I suggest doing the entire ride on your small blade.

Improve your time trial

Start with a 20-minute warm-up at a high cadence, then throw in a series of long intervals (4–5 minutes) at your goal race pace, followed by a gentle recovery. You can do multiple sets of intervals depending on your fitness level. The longer the race, the longer the race pace interval i.e. if you're training for Ironman, introduce intervals of 20 minutes or more.

RUNNING TRAINING

There is little doubt that when it comes to convenience, cost and effect, running comes out tops. A 20-minute run after work, four times a week, is all an average individual needs to class him- or herself as 'fit'. My experience at Runner's World has allowed me to learn much about this particular discipline from many top athletes, coaches and colleagues. By far the most important of all these lessons is to build proper, effective mileage. The key to good running training in triathlon lies in three basic areas:

1. Stick to the rule of only increasing your time/mileage by 10% every week.
2. Ensure you have the correct shoes.
3. Learn to run on 'dead legs'.

Running may be the most natural of all the three triathlon disciplines but it is arguably the most difficult to master. That's not surprising since it comes at the end of a hard swim and tough cycle, and you are forced to run on fatigued legs – which often accentuates biomechanical problems.

Because of its jarring nature, running is often given a bad name ... dodgy knees, creaky hip joints, a sore back. The detractors of running will blame the sport, not the athlete. In truth, studies have shown that knees, hips and backs don't degenerate through running unless it is done in excess and without suitable cushioning and support. Novice runners suffer the most: they start a running programme and rapidly gain cardiovascular fitness, but their knees, muscles and joints often take longer to adapt. Soon they're trying to run like a marathoner – and end up with injuries.

Therefore, it is vital that build-up is gradual and that the 10% weekly increase in training is always adhered to. Many experts suggest that every third running week be one of consolidation during which no increases are made. If your strength is swimming or cycling and you are new to running, take extra care since your cardiovascular fitness may allow you to run too much, too soon. Ideally, anybody new to running should start with a gentle run/walk programme of only 20 minutes at a time, moving up from there.

RIGHT *Workouts that build strength in running are vital in triathlon. Step work builds leg speed and strength all in one go.*

It is obvious: running after cycling is harder than running with a fresh set of legs – but it is that first 500m (550yd) of any running leg that is the most rewarding for the triathlete in terms of physical challenge. Your legs feel like jelly, your quadriceps are tight from the cycle phase and your body is fatigued. It is the moment of truth in the triathlon when your body tells you to give up or carry on, whether you're at the back of the field or winging it with the top athletes upfront. It is when the mind is forced to overpower the body and make it do something it normally wouldn't. But just as soon as you're feeling that you'll never be able to continue, your body adapts. Your previously dormant hamstrings (the dominant running muscles that provide power and lift) suddenly take over the tired quadriceps and you begin to transform from cyclist to runner. Understand that generally, after the cycle leg, you won't ever run as quickly as you would in a separate road-running race.

How to be a better triathlon runner

Strength

Triathlon running is less about speed and more about strength. At world-class level, an elite road runner will run 10km (6.2 miles) in 27–29 minutes, while at world triathlon level, these times drop to 30–31 minutes.

The key to a good running leg is strength – but it concerns upper body and abdominal strength as well. If your body is fatigued and your core abdominal strength weak, the run will also be weak. To be a successful triathlon runner, it is crucial to include at least two sessions a week of abdominal and back work in your workouts (see Resistance Training pp43–45).

Bike to run transition

It's a simple tip: at the end of the cycle leg, increase your leg speed. This will loosen up the hamstrings and quads, and will make the run transition easier.

Practise it

The best way to improve your bike-to-run transition is to practise. In the final few weeks before a goal race, practise your transitions by doing a 'brick' session in which you string a cycle and a run back to back. You can do multiple cycle-run sessions in one training stint depending on your level of fitness.

Relax

Much has been written about the 'correct way to run'. In essence, it is difficult to define a correct way since everyone has a different style – but this can be honed and perfected through a combination of long slow runs, tempo runs and speedwork.

THE ACTIVE STRETCH ROUTINE

Active stretches work on strengthening muscles rather than improving flexibility. In triathletes, an effective range of motion depends on how strongly the muscles contract to move the limbs fast during competition. Known as eccentric contraction, this involves tension in the muscle at the same time it is being stretched (lengthened).

1 SQUAT STRETCH

For: cycling. Actively stretches the Achilles tendon and quadriceps.

❶ Stand upright, feet hip width apart. Squat slowly, flexing knees and keeping spine straight as torso moves forward. Heels should stay in contact with floor with thighs almost parallel to the ground. Rise slowly, relax, then repeat. Keep knees over feet to prevent knee injury.

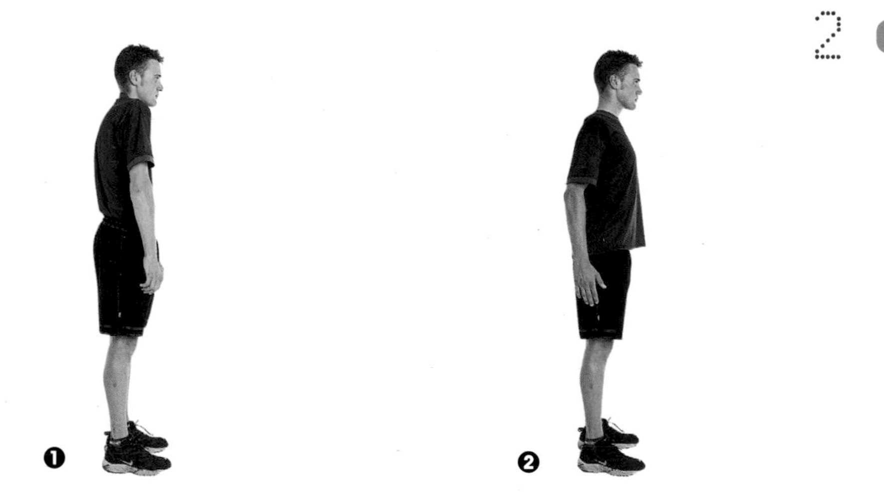

2 SHOULDER STRETCH

For: recovery movement-swimming. Protraction and retraction stretch shoulders and shoulder girdle.

❶ Stand straight, relaxed, arms at your sides. Round shoulders to rotate them as far forward as possible.

❷ Rotate shoulders back as far as you can, pushing chest forward. Keep the motion only in the shoulders.

3 HEEL RAISE

For: running. Full ankle-joint extension to promote a full push-off.

❶ Stand (0.5–1m; 2–4ft) from a wall and rest your hands against it, slightly above shoulder height, with arms extended. Your heels will rise off the ground.

❷ Lower heels to the ground (or lean towards the wall) to stretch the muscles and tendons. Hold for 2 seconds, rise on balls of feet, hold for 2 seconds. Repeat.

LUNGE

4

For: running. Stretches hip flexor muscles for greater stride length.

❶ Stand, feet hip-width apart, and take a large step forward, toes facing straight. Keep back leg extended, weight on front leg, and sink down with an upright torso.

❷ Hold for 2 seconds to feel stretch in hip flexors, then return to standing position by pushing back with front leg. Repeat with other leg.

'SUPERMAN'

5

For: cycling. Stretches abdominals and reverses rounded back from cycling.

❶ Lie face down on the floor, with arms and legs stretched straight out. Simultaneously raise the arms and legs to extend the spine.

Hold, then slowly lower to the floor. If you are struggling to do this, raise only the arms, or legs, at a time.

ARM RAISE

6

For: swimming. Loosens the shoulder joints and moves the scapula through its full range of motion for the stroke recovery phase.

❶ Stand upright, arms hanging straight alongside your torso. Extend arms out to the side, then stretch straight above the shoulders as high as possible.

❷ Return straight arms slowly to your sides, pause, then repeat.

RUN WORKOUTS

To build endurance

Just like in cycling, the importance of the weekly long run cannot be overemphasized. But, unlike cycling, you need to build it up slowly. Take your longest mid-week run and lengthen it by 30% for your long weekend run. Then increase this by only 10% each week thereafter, making sure to consolidate every third week. The long run should always be slow and easy.

To run better off the bike

Do a back-to-back 'brick' session: try 15 minutes of cycling followed by five minutes of running. Do this three times and you create a quality triathlon-specific hour of training for yourself.

To build speed and endurance

Referred to as 400s, this is an old running classic. After a short warm-up, run three to four 400m sets at your goal 10km race pace (three to four 440yd sets at 6-mile pace). Make sure you recover fully in-between each session so you don't lose form.

To build strength

Hill sessions are not only good for building power and strength, they also improve speed. After a short warm-up, find a hill that's between 60 and 80m (65–85yd) long. Run each uphill at 90% effort and recover by walking downhill slowly. Recover with a slow jog home.

To build form

In triathlon, maintaining a relaxed form is key to a good run leg. Practise this session: warm up, then do 10 short 10-second strides, concentrating on not tensing the upper body and taking strong powerful strides. Each 10-second burst should start slowly and build up to 5km (3-mile) race pace. Recover fully between each burst.

HAMISH CARTER

Looking for gold

In a sport that has its fair share of Australians, New Zealand's Hamish Carter has been a thorn in the side of his cousins up north in triathlon's Olympic Distance since the early 1990s. Born in Auckland in 1971, Carter, as a rower at national level, always had the overall body strength and endurance to make it as a triathlete. After competing in his first triathlon in 1991, he finished third in his first New Zealand championships and was promptly whisked away to Europe by a group of Australian triathletes.

He made a dramatic entry into world-class competition when he finished third at the 1993 ITU World Championships in Manchester, UK.

He was ranked number one by the International Triathlon Union in 2002 after placing consistently high in World Cup events. Carter's biggest disappointment, perhaps, was his 26th place in 2000 at the inaugural Olympic triathlon in Sydney, where he was competing in front of a strongly supportive and patriotic crowd. But his bronze at the 2002 Commonwealth Games proved that he was still a force to be reckoned with.

Despite his disheartening performance in Australia's capital, Carter has in recent years been the most consistent Olympic distance triathlete. In 1997, he won twice on the fiercely competitive ITU circuit, followed by another two wins in 1998, and a win each in 1999 and 2000. A significant first place was in the 1998 ITU World Cup race in his hometown, Auckland. After his third place in 2002 at the Commonwealth Games, the only thing missing from Hamish Carter's long list of achievements was a world championship gold.

His experiences as a triathlete have nudged him into a post-triathlon career very different from his first career choice as engineer. Thanks to his positive experiences of the profession through his own personal achievements, Carter hopes to become a sports psychologist. In the meanwhile, the Auckland resident has put his country on the international triathlon map and spawned the development of a new wave of New Zealand triathletes.

'When you win, you know you've done it on your own. That's kinda neat.'

— Hamish Carter, on the individual aspect of triathlon

TRANSITIONS

A fast transition is less important at the back of a triathlon field than among the elites, but at some point in a triathlete's career, the importance of slicing a few minutes from a race time will become critical. A fast transition is possible for everyone – with a bit of practice and some useful equipment, anyone can improve their transition times.

T1 (Swim to bike)

Get set

During the swim section, because most of the blood in the body is being pumped to the shoulders and arms, it is important to get the legs activated as soon as possible. To do this, increase your kick over the final few metres of the swim leg. This forces blood into the leg muscles and makes them better able to handle the effort when you do hit land.

Lube up

Before putting on your wetsuit, use a nonpetroleum-based lubricant on your forearms and wrists, and on your lower legs, ankles and feet. Cooking oil will even do the trick! This not only helps you slide on your wetsuit, it also helps when you remove it in a hurry at the end of the swim.

Be prepared

If you're in a wetsuit, start removing the arms and upper body of the suit as soon as you exit the water. Then, once you've reached the transition point, remove the rest of the wetsuit by using one leg to hold the suit down while you pull the other leg out. As you're doing this, you can start putting on your cycling helmet and sunglasses.

Tri cycling shoes

You can either buy specific triathlon shoes, which have only one or two Velcro straps across the shoes, or adapt your standard multiple-strap shoes by removing the tongue and the middle strap. The fewer straps you have on your cycling shoes, the easier it is to fasten them on the cycle leg.

Cleat attachment

Before you even start the swim leg, attach your cycling shoes to your cycling cleats. Once you've exited transition, you can start pedalling with your feet on top of the shoes, then slide your feet in once you've got some momentum. This is much easier than wasting time in transition.

Accessories

How serious you are about your race will depend on how many accessories you put into your transition area. Always lay out your shoes, glasses, energy bars, etc. in an orderly fashion – but be prepared, you may have to look around if some of the competitors have disrupted your layout in the excitement of the race. For this reason, it's always a good idea to get to a triathlon as early as possible. That way you can find a good position in the transition area instead of having to put up with the dregs just before the race start.

T2 (Bike to run)

Geography

Always find a landmark near your transition area in order to make a mental note of where you are located, cross-referencing it to the water exit and cycle entry area. I have seen too many headless chickens in a transition area to know that 'losing' your gear is one of the most common novice triathlete mistakes.

Practice

Once you have racked your bike, make a few runs up from the water where you will be looking for the bike to help you remember its location. Before the race, it is a good idea to take your bike outside with your helmet and shoes. Practise running up to your bike, fastening your helmet and putting your shoes on (if you do not leave them on the bike, that is). You could even time yourself to spur you on!

Racers

Ideally, the triathlete should wear light, flexible racing shoes that are roomy and spacious. Always prepare your shoes for triathlon by pulling the tongue out and down. For the recreational triathlete, specialized racing shoes are optional.

Remove and run

As you approach the transition area, remove your feet from your cycling shoes and put your feet on top of the shoes. Once you hit the transition area, all you need do is hop off your bike and head for your running apparel.

Toggles and elastic laces

Buy both or at least one. Toggles are designed for easy tightening – feed your laces through them and by pulling them up, you instantly tighten up. Elastic laces work perfectly when tightened correctly. The triathlete stretches open the shoes, then lets go for an instant fit.

Spin

During the final kilometre of your ride, increase your pedal speed (cadence). This will help to activate the hamstring muscles and clear out any lactic acid you've built up during the cycle leg.

A good suggestion is to allocate some time in the day to practise for 30 minutes before going through the motions of the real transition. It will not go wasted.

4 TACKLING YOUR TRAINING

Triathlon is sexy. Why? Because there is no other sport that produces the Greek god (and goddess) physiques that muscle around the world's transition areas. In the world of sport, a well-conditioned triathlon body – strong, lean and muscular – is the perfect specimen of a balanced body shape. It embodies the classic male and female form. There is nothing more impressive than German Ironman contender Norman Stadler's powerful tanned and shaven legs in full motion on his bike; or the graceful long, lithe legs of Australian Olympic Distance specialist Michellie Jones in running mode.

The reasons for this powerful body-sculpting are simple. Because triathletes must swim, cycle and run, they get the benefit of working all three sets of muscles. Swimming strengthens the back and shoulders, cycling produces powerful quads, and running, defined hamstrings. As a result, triathletes rarely get injured. Where the individual sports of running, cycling and swimming often cause the participants to suffer injuries through simple overuse of the muscles, triathletes are able to take time off from one discipline and concentrate on tho other two if a niggling irritation appears. Triathlon is also a forgiving sport, no matter what your level of ability is. Some triathletes are hopeless in the water but superb on the bike and run legs of a race, while others specialize in opening up a gap for themselves in the water but just holding out when the race hits land.

The question is, how do triathletes keep up interest levels in such strenuous activity? The secret is to listen to any of the world's most successful sportsmen and women – almost all of them will tell you that the secret to their success is the continuing enjoyment in their particular sport. Even in sports that offer their stars huge financial returns, people like golfer Tiger Woods, for example, attribute their success to a love of the sport rather than the financial reward.

And so it is with triathlon at all levels. In introducing you here to some of the many different triathlon training styles and programmes, the key to their success is how they make the triathlete feel. If training becomes tedious, boring and regimented it has no chance of succeeding. So never follow a training regime that does not inspire, energize and motivate you.

BODY AND MIND

Training serves two purposes. Firstly, it conditions the body to accept a higher workload, increases cardiovascular function and, with correct rest, strengthens the body. The second positive effect is a mental one. Training builds confidence. The more you train, the more you believe in your ability to perform well during a race ('I've trained, therefore I will do well'). So your mental attitude towards it is as important as the effort itself. Top US running and triathlon coach Bobby McGee is a strong advocate for mental training and believes that mental strength is just as important as physical fitness.

It is therefore important to see training as consisting of two elements and to realize how important both are when it comes to testing out that training in competition. Emotionally, long training rides instil the confidence to tackle any distance; short fast time-trial runs are exhilarating as well as confidence-boosting; and tough sets of hard swimming teach mental resilience for the rigours of a competition swim. It figures, then, that mental and emotional rest is as important as physical rest. It is a frequent occurrence that, after a long hard build-up to a major race, triathletes simply lose the desire to train. There is no reason to question this – it is your body's natural way of forcing you to take your foot off the accelerator.

In this chapter you will be introduced to a variety of training programmes, ranging from taking your first step in triathlon to tackling your second or third Ironman. Giving you physical schedules to follow, you have to work out what the mental and emotional effects of that training will create for you personally. For example: if day four of your eight-week training programme for a Sprint Distance triathlon includes a 30km (18.6-mile) bicycle ride but is coupled with a tough day at the office and a potential clash with your best friend, then you need to relook at the schedule and decide whether this is one session worth missing. If you force yourself to do it when you aren't mentally able to enjoy the experience, it's probably better to give it a miss.

Most training tables are based on the need to attain a certain effort level, measured as a percentage of your personal effort output (e.g. you may be required to do a run at 70% of maximum effort). This is more easily achieved using a heart-rate monitor. By recording your maximum heart rate in a watch that is electromagnetically connected to a transmitter worn as a band around the chest, you can measure your pulse rate during a run. Once you reach your set, or recorded, maximum the watch beeps a warning.

ABOVE *Do not underestimate the power of the mind in endurance sports: without the mental focus and determination, physical success is impossible.*

Measuring heart rate

When it comes to measuring heart rate, there are many complicated theories.

The 'age adjusted' measurement:

For men, subtract your age from 220; for women, subtract your age from 226. From this you have a predicted maximum heart rate from which to work out your various training percentages.

Karvonen equation:

This complicated method uses your heart rate reserve (the difference between your predicted maximum and your resting pulse) to calculate training zones.

Sports lab test:

You can visit a sports lab to undergo a specialized scientific test to gain an accurate heart rate measurement. Unfortunately very few triathletes will ever have the opportunity to be tested in a lab.

Maffetone method:

I firmly subscribe to the Maffetone method of working out heart rates. It is simple, easy to understand and an ideal way of ensuring that you remain healthy and injury free. After applying the formula, the figure that you arrive at will always be a safe aerobic zone at which to train. According to Maffetone's book *The High Performance Heart*:

1. Subtract your chronological age from 180.
2. Place yourself in one of four categories below:

Category A: If you have never trained before; or you are recovering from a major illness, injury or surgery; or you are taking medication, then subtract 10 from step 1.

Category B: If you have been currently exercising but are falling short of your goals e.g. improved fitness, better competitive results, more energy, better weight loss; or your workout routine is inconsistent; or you have suffered an injury; or have had two or more cases of a cold or flu in the past year – then subtract 5 from step 1.

Category C: If, for the past year, you have worked out consistently (four or more times a week), have progressed to your satisfaction (feel fitter, are enjoying better results, have more energy, increased weight loss), and have not suffered any injury or more than two colds or cases of the flu, then do not alter the number from step 1.

Category D: If you compete, and your performance has improved over the past two years, and you have not suffered any injuries or experienced more than two colds or cases of the flu, add 5 to the number obtained in step 1.

At first, your calculated safe zone may seem ridiculously low, but consistent aerobic training (specifically during the base phase of the training) within this zone will ensure steady, safe progress. Maffetone takes his theory one step further, advising that, when training, an athlete should never go outside of the above training zones. He believes that speedwork and tempo riding should be achievable in the form of aerobic intervals that don't allow the heart rate to go above its aerobic threshold.

From personal experience, and also for many triathletes, it is extremely difficult to stick to the formula – purely because it is mentally difficult to train at such a low level. On the other hand, I have seen the effects, and they work. My brother Simon, now a professional triathlete living in France and the former African triathlon champion, rarely does hard, anaerobic speedwork, yet he is capable of a sub-31-minute 10km (6.2-mile) run, and in a race situation can swim and cycle with the best of them.

When to use HRMs

Many triathletes use a heart-rate monitor (HRM) simply to gauge their effort levels. For others, the HRM is a rev counter; through technological feedback, it lets you know how your body is feeling at any given time. Then, almost in contrast to Maffetone, many top triathletes use their HRM only when doing anaerobic speedwork, to measure their recovery between intervals.

There *is* benefit in a heart-rate monitor, even without the hi-tech, scientific gobbledegook. However, I strongly believe that you should never wear an HRM during a race. Race situations are very different from the training environment, and often the excitement and adrenaline of a race elevates the heart rate much more than occurs during training. This is disconcerting to a triathlete, who may then underperform as a result of seeing his or her higher-than-normal heart rate. Race situations are not normal – and unless you are fully aware of how the stress of a race situation affects your heart rate, I would not rely on it as an accurate gauge of fitness.

MAF Test

By sticking rigidly to Maffetone's formula, it is necessary to perform his Maximum Aerobic Function, or MAF, test once every three weeks. To do this, you either cycle or run within this aerobic heart rate over a consistent predetermined course. As you progress, your times will drop but your heart rate will remain the same since your body is getting fitter and more reliant on your longer-lasting aerobic energy systems. As the graph of improvement plateaus, the athlete is then fit enough to throw in short bursts of speed, staying within the aerobic threshold, coupled with a big recovery.

Mark Allen and many of the world's best triathletes follow this hardline approach to heart-rate training. For the less serious, Maffetone's formula is a useful guideline and is arguably the most accurate in determining a proper training pace at any given time.

Triathletes and heart rate

Triathlon has initiated many new concepts into the world of sport. In 1989, cyclist Greg Lemond borrowed triathlon's aero bars, first used by Scott Tinley and Scott Molina in 1987, to beat Laurent Fignon in the final Tour de France time trial. Since that day, triathletes have always been the innovators; it is no surprise that triathletes were the first in the late 1980s to embrace the use of HRMs to better their performance. Probably the best known of the early HRM users was six-time Ironman winner Mark Allen. Under the guidance of sports physician Phil Maffetone, Allen used heart-rate training to great effect in the early 1990s, and both he and Maffetone revolutionized the way HRMs were used.

TIME MANAGEMENT

Triathlon is tough – it takes many hours of dedicated training to reach even a mediocre standard of competence, for the simple reason that there are three disciplines making up one sport. As a triathlete with a wife, two children and a full-time job, I have slowly realized that my lifestyle will never allow me to reach my full potential. So my sport has become my hobby; I can only try to be the best I can under the circumstances. Time with my family is important, as is my job, so triathlon lies in solid third position on my list of priorities.

To be truly great in a sport requires immense personal sacrifice. Top triathletes are often social outcasts; they rarely socialize with friends as they're usually too tired after training. Their lives revolve around what is, essentially, a selfish pastime. But you shouldn't let this put you off. It is possible to be a competitive triathlete even if you're distracted by the many other priorities in your life. Try these tricks to make the most of your training time.

Get it done early

If you work a normal nine-to-five job, the best time to train is in the morning when the rest of the family is asleep. Never assume that you'll get in a session later; once the day gets going, you will often simply run out of time. Early morning training is also invigorating and relaxing ahead of a day of responsibilities.

Consistency counts

Top coaches stress the importance of consistent training: 30 minutes every day is better than an hour every second day – or a 90-minute session every third day. Personally, during peak times of stress I set myself a goal of at least 20 minutes a day. If I'm busy, I'll sneak out of the office at lunchtime or I'll spend that time on the wind trainer at home while the children are in the bath. It may not seem like much but it keeps me on track.

Get your partner to 'buy in'

It may seem a bit silly, but when it comes to training, get your life-partner to 'buy into' your plans. A friend of mine concentrates on one major event a year and although he trains all year around, he knuckles down seriously eight weeks before the event. Beforehand, he sits down with his wife and explains his plan and, between the two of them, they find time for his training. Once your partner knows that there's a defined goal, it'll be much easier for them to accept that you're not going to be there to snuggle up to on Sunday mornings.

Be realistic

Before embarking on a triathlon training programme, be realistic about your life and your ability. Work out exactly how much training you can comfortably do in a week and build on that. Take into account your job and your commitment to family and friends. Then see how you can use the rest of the available time.

KEEPING A BASIC LOGBOOK

Call it a logbook or a training diary, this is almost as important as the training itself. A logbook serves two purposes.

1. It provides the triathlete with an accurate record of training before a major event.
2. It is probably the cheapest and most effective motivational tool on the market.

By keeping an accurate record of your training, your state of health, your daily heart rate and the conditions under which you train, it is easier to see what effect that training has had on your overall performance. Without this record, preparation for your goal race will be haphazard and unstructured, and can lead to a lack of performance and possible injury. The human mind has a short memory when it comes to physical stress and often the rigours of a hard session will be forgotten sooner than the body can recover – which is why it is best to record it.

It is as a motivational tool, however, that the logbook comes into its own. Making a note of each training session, then planning ahead, means you continually tick off successful sessions. Each tick adds to your motivation and leaves a smile on your face.

How to structure a logbook

Many triathletes make the mistake of simply noting the training session they did on a given day, rather than focusing on a long-term goal. So before you embark on keeping a daily training journal, *have a plan*.

Set yourself a goal race, then work back from the race date. Determine exactly how many weeks you have to train, then work backwards starting with the taper, then the speed and tempo phases of the programme, ending with the base phase of your training. In this way, you can accurately apportion the vital elements of your training programme into the time you have available. Also, set yourself daily goals.

Danger signs

Be flexible:

You must ensure that you control the diary, and the diary doesn't control you. One of the most common mistakes made by athletes in endurance sports is to focus solely on completing each training session without taking fatigue, illness and stress into account. It is good to have goals, but the logbook is merely a guide. If your log dictates that you complete a 1500m (0.9-mile) swim and hard 40km (25-mile) cycle on a Saturday morning but you've been up all night looking after a sick child, then re-assess the session.

More equals less:

Often optimum training is based on a programme that allows good recovery between sessions so that the triathlete remains healthy and motivated. It doesn't work to try to do more in the hope that you will perform better.

Triathlon specifics

Unlike a single-sport diary, the triathlon diary is a far more complicated journal. You need to include the following elements:

Morning/resting pulse rate:

This is an ideal indicator of your day-to-day fitness and state of health. You can either use a heart-rate monitor or do the pulse test just after you wake up in the morning (find your pulse with your finger and count the beats for 10 seconds, then multiply that number by six). A heart rate that is 10 or more beats per minute higher than your normal rate indicates sickness or overtraining.

Record the details:

Make detailed notes of each swim, bike or run section: the time of day you did the training, the weather conditions, the distance or time completed and the effort level or average.

Mood indicator:

Give yourself a mood indicator from 1 to 10 – 1 means you're feeling lousy and battling with illness or injury, 5 means you're not 100% but could probably manage an easy session, while 10 means you're ready for anything. You'd be surprised how accurate your own assessment can be.

Simple training truths

- Don't suddenly increase your mileage because you've read what Ironman champion Peter Reid does over a weekend. Only increase your time/mileage by 10% each week; also, consolidate every third week.
- Don't set yourself lofty goals that you're unlikely to achieve; you'll be disappointed and demotivated. By setting realistic training and racing goals, you'll be able to tick off successes that will inspire you.
- If you're built like a Sumo wrestler, don't expect to race like a greyhound. You can only be the best you can be – accept that and you'll be a happy triathlete.
- Be creative. A good triathlete will always come up with creative ways of training – with some thought and mind power, even the busiest people can do enough to keep them enjoying the sport, and not finding excuses as to why they shouldn't train on any given day.

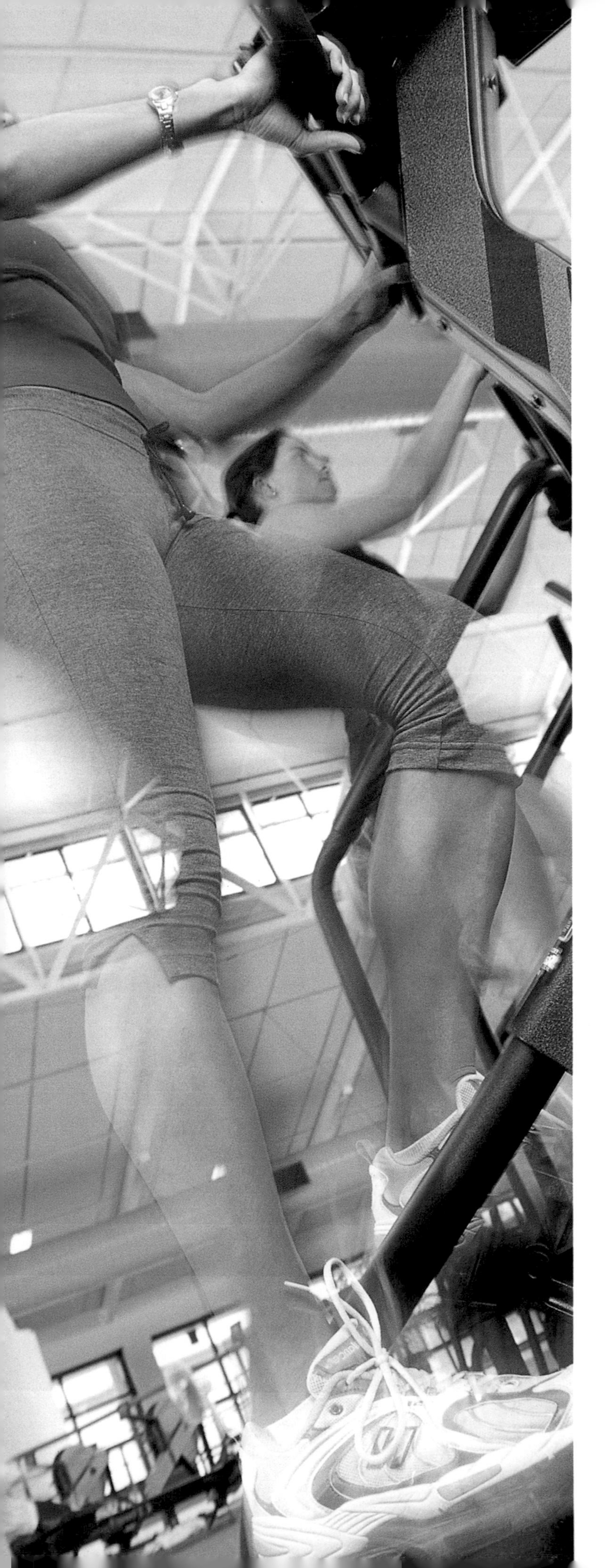

CYCLIC TRAINING

In any endurance sport – and particularly in triathlon – there are three distinct development phases, followed by a tapering phase (note how training effort is tapered off in the last week – or couple of weeks – of the training programmes that follow in this chapter). The phases are:

1. Base training
2. Tempo training
3. Speedwork
4. Tapering.

Base training

Also known as steady state training, base training is the foundation of any proper training programme. On the face of it, base training is easy. It is done at a perceived easy and moderate effort level (typically between 60–75% of maximum heart rate) and helps the body adapt slowly to the rigours of training. During this phase, the body relies primarily on stored body fat, which metabolizes slowly. It is therefore the most effective zone for losing weight.

Advantages

Base training is all about consistency and time. Slow increments in time or distance (not more than a 10% increase per week in time or distance is recommended) help strengthen muscles, tendons and ligaments so that they can handle the rigours of faster, more vigorous training.

Disadvantages

Mentally, base training is the toughest phase of the training pyramid. Forcing yourself to cycle slowly and deliberately is often much harder mentally than an adrenaline-pumping flat-out session with your mates. This is the reason why many triathletes fail to reach their true potential – they simply battle to do enough slow, easy, steady-state training.

Tempo training

Without base training, tempo training operates on shaky ground. It is performed at a higher intensity, and is shorter and more specific in design: you could build in two to three tempo sessions a week where you swim at your 1500m (0.9-mile) race pace, but over a shorter distance or broken up into sets. The idea is to help the body become accustomed to race pace while maintaining good form.

Typically, tempo pace refers to your Olympic Distance race pace – or between 70 and 85% of your maximum heart rate. In other words, a tempo swim session will include 4 x 100m at your 1500m (0.9-mile) race pace; or a bike ride that includes intervals of 5 minutes at your 40km (25-mile) time trial effort; or a run session that includes 5 x 400m at your 10km race pace (5 x 440yd at 6-mile pace).

Tempo training is never done flat out, but your breathing will be hard. Using a heart-rate monitor is an ideal way to keep an eye on your effort without the guesswork.

Speedwork

This is the final tune-up. In the build-up to a major race, a triathlete will only bring in speedwork for the final third of the training programme. Unless properly worked into your training, speedwork is dangerous for two reasons:

- **Firstly**, done too often and at a high intensity, injury is inevitable.
- **Secondly**, it is tempting to do too much, and neglect your tempo/base work. Ideally, you don't want to do more than one speed session per week per discipline – this is all the body needs to improve on speed. Speed sessions are useless if done while you're tired, and there is no benefit if you follow with another hard session the day after. Always do an easy routine both before and after a speed workout.

The training programmes

Presented here is a series of training programmes for everyone from beginner Sprint Distance to Ironman competitor. The advice of three training coaches has been sought. A few of the programmes come from American Hazen Kent, whose prime ambition is to ensure that whoever uses them, enjoys the experience. Being healthy and injury-free is the overriding message put out by his website – and so it should be in any triathlete's life. Also included is an intermediate Sprint Distance training programme from US Triathlon National Teams Program Director, Libby Burrell, and an Ironman competition programme from top South African coach, competitor and physiotherapist Lou-Anne Rivett. These programmes can be adapted to suit each individual. Training for a Sprint Distance triathlon is vastly different to training for an Ironman event, and particularly for the 'newbie' it is vital to move slowly up the ladder before attempting such an event. The training programmes follow.

Remember the basics

- Avoid doing too much too soon; over-enthusiasm early in your training often leads to athletes opting out.
- Stick to your plan.
- Control the pace of each session according to your predetermined plan.
- In the beginning, plan your sessions according to time (duration) rather than distance.
- Make sure your training is FUN – this will help you to keep at it.

1-4

GETTING DOWN TO THE NITTY-GRITTY

Training Programmes

Zero to hero in 11 weeks (beginners):
Sprint Distance
8 weeks (experienced):
Sprint Distance
11 weeks (beginners):
Standard/Olympic Distance
18 weeks (experienced):
Standard/Olympic Distance

Actually taking the plunge into full training mode can feel like a formidable task, especially for beginners, so the training programmes here are divided into two sections. The first section takes the novice triathlete through a comprehensive beginner programme for the Sprint Distance, culminating with a Standard/Olympic programme.

The second section tackles the real hardcore events – the Half and full distance Ironman challenges – an entry to which demands hard training, strength and commitment.

PROGRAMME 1:

Zero to hero in 11 weeks

by Hazen Kent; www.trinewbies.com

Sprint distance

750m swim, 20km cycle, 5km run

(0.5 mile; 12.4 miles; 3.1 miles)

If you're new to triathlon, this is the programme for you. It is a survival programme to get you through your first triathlon, and time is not an issue. The entire starting programme should be done at a low range of effort. It's not about how fast you go; it's that you complete the training distances comfortably. All the swimming should be done using the freestyle stroke, although you can break down each section into manageable segments to keep things interesting.

Week 1

	Swim	Cycle	Run
Monday	Rest	Rest	Rest
Tuesday	—	—	2km (1M*)
Wednesday	—	8km (5M)	—
Thursday	200m crawl	—	—
Friday	Rest	Rest	Rest
Saturday	—	—	2km (1M)
Sunday	—	8km (5M)	—

Week 2

	Swim	Cycle	Run
Monday	Rest	Rest	Rest
Tuesday	200m crawl [A.M.]	—	2km (1M) [P.M.]
Wednesday	—	8km (5M)	—
Thursday	200m	—	—
Friday	Rest	Rest	Rest
Saturday	—	—	3km (2M)
Sunday	—	10km (6M)	—

Week 3

	Swim	Cycle	Run
Monday	Rest	Rest	Rest
Tuesday	200m [A.M.]	—	2km (1M) [P.M.]
Wednesday	—	8km (5M)	—
Thursday	300m [A.M.]	—	Walk 30 min. [P.M.]
Friday	Rest	Rest	Rest
Saturday	—	—	4km (2.5M)
Sunday	—	13km (8M)	—

*M = Mile

Week 4

	Swim	Cycle	Run
Monday	Rest	Rest	Rest
Tuesday	300m [A.M.]	—	2km (1M) [P.M.]
Wednesday	—	8km (5M)	—
Thursday	300m [A.M.]	—	Walk 30 min. [P.M.]
Friday	Rest	Rest	Rest
Saturday	—	—	5km (3M)
Sunday	—	16km (10M)	—

Week 5

	Swim	Cycle	Run
Monday	Rest	Rest	Rest
Tuesday	300m [A.M.]	—	3km (2M) [P.M.]
Wednesday	—	8km (5M)	—
Thursday	400m [A.M.]	—	Walk 30 min. [P.M.]
Friday	Rest	Rest	Rest
Saturday	—	—	5km (3M)
Sunday	—	20km (12M)	—

Week 6

	Swim	Cycle	Run
Monday	Rest	Rest	Rest
Tuesday	400m [A.M.]		4km (2.5M) [P.M.]
Wednesday		8km (5M)	
Thursday	400m [A.M.]		Walk 45 min. [P.M.]
Friday	Rest	Rest	Rest
Saturday	—		5km (3M)
Sunday	—	25km (15.5M)	—

Week 7

	Swim	Cycle	Run
Monday	Rest	Rest	Rest
Tuesday	400m [A.M.]	—	3km (2M) [P.M.]
Wednesday	—	16km (10M)	—
Thursday	500m [A.M.]	—	Walk 45 min. [P.M.]
Friday	Rest	Rest	Rest
Saturday	—	—	6km (4M)
Sunday	—	25km (15.5M) [A.M.]	Walk 30 min. [P.M.]

Week 8

	Swim	Cycle	Run
Monday	Rest	Rest	Rest
Tuesday	500m [A.M.]	—	3km (2M) [P.M.]
Wednesday	—	16km (10M)	—
Thursday	500m [A.M.]	—	Walk 45 min. [P.M.]
Friday	Rest	Rest	Rest
Saturday	—	—	6km (4M)
Sunday	—	30km (18.5M) [A.M.]	Walk 30 min. [P.M.]

Week 9

	Swim	Cycle	Run
Monday	Rest	Rest	Rest
Tuesday	500m [A.M.]	—	5km (3M) [P.M.]
Wednesday	—	25km (15.5M)	—
Thursday	600m [A.M.]	—	Walk 45 min. [P.M.]
Friday	Rest	Rest	Rest
Saturday	—	—	6km (4M)
Sunday	—	30km (18.5M)	Walk 30 min.

Week 10

	Swim	Cycle	Run
Monday	Rest	Rest	Rest
Tuesday	600m [A.M.]	—	5km (3M) [P.M.]
Wednesday	—	25km (15.5M)	—
Thursday	600m [A.M.]	—	Walk 45 min. [P.M.]
Friday	Rest	Rest	Rest
Saturday	—	—	8km (5M)
Sunday	—	30km (18.5M) [A.M.]	Walk 30 min. [P.M.]

Week 11 RACE WEEK

	Swim	Cycle	Run
Monday	Rest	Rest	Rest
Tuesday	500m [A.M.]	—	5km (3M) [P.M.]
Wednesday	—	20km (12M)	—
Thursday	200m [A.M.]	—	2km (1M) [P.M.]
Friday	Rest	Rest	Rest
Saturday	RACE DAY		

PROGRAMME 2:

8 weeks (experienced)

by Libby Burrell
USA Triathlon National Programs Director

Sprint distance

750m swim, 20km cycle, 5km run
(0.5 mile; 12.4 miles; 3.1 miles)

In the training outline that follows, in each of the three disciplines there is one long controlled-pace session and one specific session (tempo, interval, or medium- or race-pace session) depending on the phase of training you are in (Base Building, Intensity or Race Phase). This programme focuses on time (length of effort) rather than distance – an excellent way to concentrate on your form and physical state rather than average speeds and distances. I'd recommend removing the cycling computer from your bike and simply using a stopwatch to train with.

Am I ready?

To attempt this programme you should have completed at least five Sprint Distance triathlons, be able to swim 45 minutes at a stretch, ride for 90 minutes plus run for one hour continuously.

Week 1: Focus on distance at a controlled pace (Base Building Phase).
Weeks 4–6: More specific sessions (tempo, intensity or race pace sessions) still maintaining a distance focus (Intensity Phase).
Weeks 6–8: Focus on racing (Race Phase).

Week 1

	Swim	Cycle	Run
Monday	Group session: 45 min.	—	—
Tuesday	—	Group ride on a hilly route: 60 min.	—
Wednesday	—	—	Easy run: 35 min.
Thursday	Group session: 45 min.	—	—
Friday	Rest	Rest	Rest
Saturday	—	LSD 90 min.	—
Sunday	—	—	LSD 60 min.

Week 2

	Swim	Cycle	Run
Monday	Group session: 50 min.	—	—
Tuesday	—	Group ride on a hilly route: 60 min.	—
Wednesday	—	—	Easy run: 35 min.
Thursday	Group session: 50 min.	—	—
Friday	Rest	Rest	Rest
Saturday	—	LSD 90 min.	—
Sunday	—	—	LSD 65 min.

Week 3

	Swim	Cycle	Run
Monday	Group session: 60 min.	—	—
Tuesday	—	Group ride on a hilly route: 60 min.	—
Wednesday	—	—	Easy run: 35 min.
Thursday	Group session: 60 min.	—	—
Friday	Rest	Rest	Rest
Saturday	—	LSD 90 min.	—
Sunday	—	—	LSD 60 min.

Week 4

	Swim	Cycle	Run
Monday	Group session: 60 min.	—	—
Tuesday	—	Tempo session: ride 4 x 5 min. at 20km (6M) race pace	—
Wednesday	—	—	Tempo run: 3 x 5 min. at 5–10 sec. slower than 10km (6M) race pace
Thursday	Group session: 60 min.	—	—
Friday	Rest	Rest	Rest
Saturday	—	LSD 90 min.	—
Sunday	—	—	LSD 70 min.

Week 5

	Swim	Cycle	Run
Monday	Group session: 60 min.	—	—
Tuesday	—	Tempo session: ride 2 x 10 min. at 20km (12M) race pace	—
Wednesday	—	—	Tempo run: 5 x 5 min. at 5–10 sec. slower than 10km (6M) race pace
Thursday	Group Session: 60 min.	—	—
Friday	Rest	Rest	Rest
Saturday	—	LSD 90 min.	—
Sunday	—	—	LSD 75 min.

Week 6

	Swim	Cycle	Run
Monday	Group session: 60 min.	—	—
Tuesday	—	Race session: ride 30km (18.5M) at race pace	—
Wednesday	—	—	Tempo run: 5 x 5 min. at 5–10 sec. slower than 10km (6M) race pace
Thursday	Group session: 1000m time trial	—	—
Friday	Rest	Rest	Rest
Saturday	—	LSD 90 min.	
Sunday	—	—	LSD 60 min.

Week 7

	Swim	Cycle	Run
Monday	Group session: 60 min.	—	—
Tuesday	—	Race session: ride 2 x 10km (6M) at race pace. Spin 5km between 10km bouts (3M, 6M)	—
Wednesday	—	—	Race pace: run 1 x 5km (3M)
Thursday	Group session: 60 min.	—	—
Friday	Rest	Rest	Rest
Saturday	500m at race pace	60 min. at controlled pace	—
Sunday	—	—	LSD 60 min.

Should you train the day before?

If done at the right intensity and duration, training the day before a goal Half Standard triathlon will make a big difference to your race day performance. Why? The body's nervous system needs to be activated to be ready for the race – and the best way to achieve this is to stimulate the body to perform at your expected race pace without putting it under undue stress. A gentle warm-up on the bike followed by a series of short race-pace bursts does just enough to stimulate the nervous system at the right intensity. You can do the same in both swimming and running. Exercise the day before a race also pumps blood through the muscles, loosening ligaments while also helping store carbohydrates in your muscles.

Week 8

RACE WEEK

	Swim	Cycle	Run
Monday	Group session: 45 min.	—	—
Tuesday	—	Race session: ride 1 x 10km (6M) at race pace	
Wednesday	—	—	Race session: run 3 x 1km (0.5M) at race pace with long rests between repeats
Thursday	Group session: 45 min.	—	—
Friday	Rest	Rest	Rest
Saturday	Easy swim: 800m; include 4 x 50m at race pace	Warm up: ride 5–10km (6M) easy; include 4 x 30 sec. fast	Warm-up: run 15 min. easy; include 5 x 20 sec. fast
Sunday	RACE DAY		

PROGRAMME 3:

11-week beginners

by Hazen Kent; www.trinewbies.com

Standard/Olympic distance

1500m swim, 40km cycle, 10km run
(0.9 mile; 25 miles; 6.2 miles)

The Standard or Olympic Distance triathlon is the classical distance for triathletes, taxing both body and mind, and challenging you physically in speed and endurance. For the elite athletes, the Olympic distance is about speed – although simply completing a full Olympic Distance triathlon is a monumental achievement considering the distances involved.

For the beginner, anything between 3 and 3½ hours is a respectable time, bearing in mind the famous 2 hours 20 minutes mark as being one of the milestones in triathlon performance. Elite athletes can sometimes complete the course in under 1 hour 50 minutes!

Am I ready?

You should be able to swim 300m in one stretch, run 5km three times a week and cycle 12–16km (300m; 3 miles; 7–10 miles) without stopping.

Week 1

	Swim	Cycle	Run
Monday	Rest	Rest	Rest
Tuesday	300m [A.M.]	—	5km (3M) [P.M.]
Wednesday	—	10km (6M)	—
Thursday	300m [A.M.]	—	3km (2M) [P.M.]
Friday	Rest	Rest	Rest
Saturday	—	—	5km (3M) [A.M.]
Sunday	—	16km (10M) [A.M.]	—

Week 2

	Swim	Cycle	Run
Monday	Rest	Rest	Rest
Tuesday	300m [A.M.]		5km (3M) [P.M.]
Wednesday		16km (10M)	
Thursday	500m [A.M.]		5km (3M) [P.M.]
Friday	—	12km (7M)	—
Saturday	—	—	6km (4M)
Sunday	—	16km (10 M) [A.M.]	—

Swimming

Focus on pool drills that help you master lifting your head out of the water, so it comes naturally in open-water swimming (see Chapter 3 for more on routines).

Cycling/running

Concentrate on aerobic and tempo training. For beginners, training is all about time on the legs. Endurance, and not speed, is the essence of this programme.

Week 3

	Swim	Cycle	Run
Monday	Rest	Rest	Rest
Tuesday	500m [A.M.]	—	6km (4M) [P.M.]
Wednesday	—	16km (10M)	—
Thursday	500m [A.M.]	—	5km (3M) [P.M.]
Friday	—	16km (10M)	—
Saturday	—	—	8km (5M) [P.M.]
Sunday	—	20km (12M)	—

Week 4 RECOVERY WEEK

	Swim	Cycle	Run
Monday	Rest	Rest	Rest
Tuesday	300m [A.M.]	—	5km (3M) [P.M.]
Wednesday		10km (6M)	
Thursday	300m [A.M.]	—	5km (3M) [P.M.]
Friday	—	10km (6M)	—
Saturday	—	—	5km (3M) [A.M.]
Sunday	—	16km (10 M) [P.M.]	—

Week 5

	Swim	Cycle	Run
Monday	Rest	Rest	Rest
Tuesday	500m [A.M.]	—	6km (4M) [P.M.]
Wednesday	—	16km (10M)	—
Thursday	750m [A.M.]		5km (3M) [P.M.]
Friday	—	16km (10M)	—
Saturday	—	—	8km (5M) [A.M.]
Sunday	—	25km (5.5M) [A.M.]	—

Week 6

	Swim	Cycle	Run
Monday	Rest	Rest	Rest
Tuesday	750m [A.M.]	—	6km (4M) [P.M.]
Wednesday		25km (15.5M)	
Thursday	750m [A.M.]	—	5km (3M) [P.M.]
Friday	—	16km (10M)	—
Saturday	—	—	8km (5M) [P.M.]
Sunday	—	25km (15.5M)	—

Week 7

	Swim	Cycle	Run
Monday	Rest	Rest	Rest
Tuesday	750m [A.M.]	—	6km (4M) [P.M.]
Wednesday	—	25km (15.5M)	—
Thursday	1000m [A.M.]	—	5km (3M) [P.M.]
Friday	—	16km (10M)	—
Saturday	—	—	8km (5M) [A.M.]
Sunday	—	30km (18.5M) [A.M.]	—

Week 8 RECOVERY WEEK

	Swim	Cycle	Run
Monday	Rest	Rest	Rest
Tuesday	500m [A.M.]	—	5km (3M) [P.M.]
Wednesday		16km (10M)	
Thursday	500m [A.M.]	—	5km (3M) [P.M.]
Friday	—	16km (10M)	—
Saturday	1000m [A.M.]	—	8km (5M) [P.M.]
Sunday	—	25km (15.5M) [A.M.]	—

Week 9

	Swim	Cycle	Run
Monday	Rest	Rest	Rest
Tuesday	1000m [A.M.]	—	6km (4M) [P.M.]
Wednesday	—	25km (15.5M)	—
Thursday	1250m [A.M.]	—	6km (4M) [P.M.]
Friday	—	25km (15.5M)	—
Saturday	1000m easy optional [P.M.]	—	8km (5M) [A.M.]
Sunday	—	30km (18.5M) [A.M.]	—

From week 9 there are a few optional sessions that can be done instead of resting. If in doubt, rest; otherwise treat these sessions as easy/recovery sessions. Unlike the swim and cycle legs, all the run sessions are done according to time. It is important to stick with this, except during the quality phases of your training. Examples of quality sessions for all three disciplines appear in Chapter 3.

Don't cry over spilt milk. There are few who can ever honestly say that their training went exactly according to plan. Only the elite and very committed can go through their training without missing a beat. For most of us, our lives often get in the way. The key is not to fret over missed sessions. Analyze why you missed out and if the circumstances are beyond your control, then move on without regret.

Week 10

	Swim	Cycle	Run
Monday	Rest	Rest	Rest
Tuesday	1250m [A.M.]	—	8km (5M) [P.M.]
Wednesday		30km (18.5 M)	
Thursday	1500m [A.M.]	—	6km (4M) [P.M.]
Friday	—	25km (15.5 M)	—
Saturday	1000m easy optional [P.M.]	—	10km (6M) [A.M.]
Sunday	—	50km (30M) [A.M.]	—

Week 11

RACE WEEK

	Swim	Cycle	Run
Monday	Rest	Rest	Rest
Tuesday	1500m easy [A.M.]	—	8km (5M) easy [P.M.]
Wednesday	—	50km (30M)	—
Thursday	1000m easy [A.M.]	—	5km (3M) [P.M.]
Friday	Rest	Rest	Rest
Saturday	RACE DAY		

SIMON LESSING

The Pro

Few would argue that in his prime, Cape Town-born Englishman Simon Lessing was a cut above the rest. At his best, the tall, strongly built Lessing was powerful in each of the individual triathlon events. When he put them all together in an official triathlon race, there were few who could touch him – strong firstly in the swimming leg, Lessing was then always among the leaders heading into the bike leg and finally would blast his way through final run. In his time he has achieved a world-class 29 minutes for the 10km (6.2-mile) distance.

In his youth, Lessing, never one to accept injustice, was a fierce opponent of South Africa's apartheid system. During his school career he once removed all the duplicate books from the storeroom of his school library to give them to a nearby school for black pupils. Already a gifted runner at the time, Lessing once pulled out of a major school's athletics meeting to protest against the exclusion of a black student. He has also bumped heads with triathlon's ruling body, the ITU, on a number of occasions.

In later years, Lessing put triathlon on the UK map and was among the first Olympic distance superstars to emerge from the British pack. With a highly determined, focused character, he adapted extremely well to the new Olympic drafting format for the cycling leg, then focused on training hard for a good swim and a fast run.

He was quoted once as saying: 'To be honest, if you can't run fast you're never going to have a result in an ITU (Olympic distance series) event.'

So dominant was Simon Lessing in the 1990s that many believed all he had to do was turn up, and victory would be his. He won five ITU World Championships in all between 1992 and 1998, including a victory in 1995 in the World Long Distance Championships in Nice. Lessing's best year was probably 1998 after he won the ITU World Championships in Lausanne, then followed up with victory at the Goodwill Games. One should not count him out just yet, despite a disappointing ninth place at the 2000 Sydney Olympics after he started the race a clear favourite.

'Everything is so intense these days and the level of competition is so high that you've got to put in a higher level of commitment and work. That is literally impossible to do on your own.'

— Simon Lessing, a former loner, on the need to train with others

PROGRAMME 4:

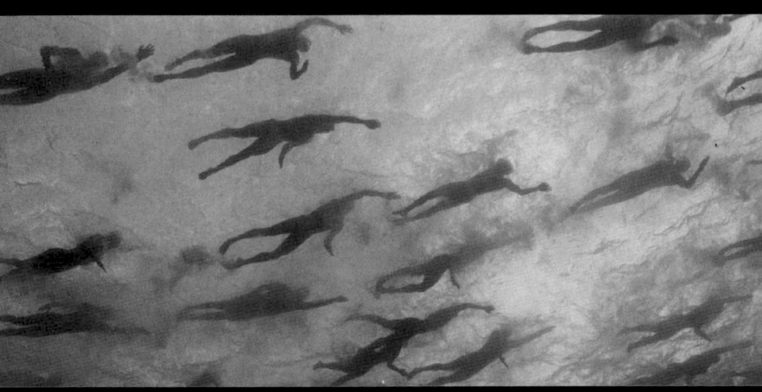

18 weeks (experienced)

by Hazen Kent; www.trinewbies.com

Standard/Olympic distance

1500m swim, 40km cycle, 10km run

(0.9 mile; 25 miles; 6.2 miles)

Once you've spent at least a season trying out a few sprint distances and a few standard distance triathlons, it may be time to step up a gear – but remember, it takes time, and it is important to be realistic about the time you have available as well as your own ability.

Week 1–12: Base building

Weeks 13–16: Speedwork/quality phase

Week 17–18: Taper

Am I ready?

Make sure you can run 8km (5 miles) in under 50 minutes, swim 3000m a week and ride 25–30km (15.5–18.5 miles) three times a week.

Week 1

	Swim	Cycle	Run
Monday	750m [A.M.]	25km (15.5M) [P.M.]	—
Tuesday	750m [A.M.]	—	20 min. [P.M.]
Wednesday	—	25km (15.5M) [A.M.]	—
Thursday	1000m [A.M.]	—	20 min. [P.M.]
Friday	Rest	Rest	Rest
Saturday	—	—	30 min. [A.M.]
Sunday	—	30km (18.5M) [A.M.]	—

Week 2

	Swim	Cycle	Run
Monday	750m [A.M.]	25km (15.5M) [P.M.]	—
Tuesday	1000m [A.M.]	—	20 min. [P.M.]
Wednesday	—	25km (15.5M) [A.M.]	—
Thursday	1250m [A.M.]	—	20 min. [P.M.]
Friday	Rest	Rest	Rest
Saturday	—	—	35 min. [A.M.]
Sunday	—	40km (25M) [A.M.]	—

Week 3

	Swim	Cycle	Run
Monday	750m [A.M.]	25km (15.5M) [P.M.]	—
Tuesday	1000m [A.M.]	—	20 min. [P.M.]
Wednesday	—	30km (18.5M) [A.M.]	—
Thursday	1500m [A.M.]	—	25 min. [P.M.]
Friday	Rest	Rest	Rest
Saturday	—	—	40 min. [A.M.]
Sunday	—	50km (30M) [A.M.]	—

Week 4 RECOVERY WEEK

	Swim	Cycle	Run
Monday	750m [A.M.]	16km (10M) [P.M.]	—
Tuesday	750m [A.M.]	—	20 min. [P.M.]
Wednesday	—	25km (15.5M) [A.M.]	—
Thursday	1250m [A.M.]	—	20 min. [P.M.]
Friday	Rest	Rest	Rest
Saturday	—	—	30 min. [P.M.]
Sunday	—	30km (18.5M) [A.M.]	—

Week 5

	Swim	Cycle	Run
Monday	1000m [A.M.]	25km (15.5M) [P.M.]	—
Tuesday	1000m [A.M.]	—	20 min. [P.M.]
Wednesday	—	30km (18.5M) [A.M.]	—
Thursday	1500m [A.M.]	—	25 min. [P.M.]
Friday	Rest	Rest	Rest
Saturday	—	—	40 min. [A.M.]
Sunday	—	50km (30M) [A.M.]	—

Week 6

	Swim	Cycle	Run
Monday	1000m [A.M.]	25km (15.5M) [P.M.]	—
Tuesday	1250m [A.M.]	—	25 min. [P.M.]
Wednesday	—	40km (25M) [A.M.]	—
Thursday	1750m [A.M.]	—	30 min.[P.M.]
Friday	Rest	Rest	Rest
Saturday	—		45 min [P.M.]
Sunday	—	60km (37M) [A.M.]	—

Week 7

	Swim	Cycle	Run
Monday	1000m [A.M.]	30km (18.5M) [P.M.]	—
Tuesday	1500m [A.M.]	—	25 min. [P.M.]
Wednesday	—	40km (25M) [A.M.]	—
Thursday	2000m [A.M.]	—	35 min. [P.M.]
Friday	Rest	Rest	Rest
Saturday	—	—	50 min. [A.M.]
Sunday	—	60km (37M)	—

Week 8 RECOVERY WEEK

	Swim	Cycle	Run
Monday	750m [A.M.]	25km (15.5M) [P.M.]	—
Tuesday	1000m [A.M.]	—	20 min. [P.M.]
Wednesday	—	30km (18.5M) [A.M.]	—
Thursday	1500m [A.M.]	—	25 min.[P.M.]
Friday	Rest	Rest	Rest
Saturday	—	—	40 min. [A.M.]
Sunday	—	50km (30M) [A.M.]	—

Week 9

	Swim	Cycle	Run
Monday	1250m [A.M.]	30km (18.5M) [P.M.]	—
Tuesday	1500m [A M.]	—	25 min. [P.M.]
Wednesday	—	40km (25M) [A.M.]	—
Thursday	2000m [A.M.]	—	35 min. [P.M.]
Friday	—	30km or rest	—
Saturday	1000m [P.M.]	—	50 min. [A.M.]
Sunday	—	60km (37M) [A.M.]	60 min. walk [P.M.] or rest

Week 10

	Swim	Cycle	Run
Monday	1500m [A.M.]	40km (25M) [P.M.]	—
Tuesday	1750m [A.M.]	—	25 min. [P.M.]
Wednesday	—	40km (25M) [A.M.]	—
Thursday	2250m [A.M.]	—	40 min. [P.M.]
Friday	—	30km (18.5M) or rest	—
Saturday	1000m [P.M.]	—	55 min. [A.M.]
Sunday	—	70km (43M) [A.M.]	60 min. walk [P.M.] or rest

Week 11

	Swim	Cycle	Run
Monday	1750m [A.M.]	40km (25M) [P.M.]	—
Tuesday	2000m [A.M.]	—	30 min. [P.M.]
Wednesday	—	50km (31M) [A.M.]	—
Thursday	2500m [A.M.]	—	45 min. [P.M.]
Friday	—	30km (18.5M)	—
Saturday	1000m [P.M.] or rest	—	60 min. [A.M.]
Sunday	—	80km (50M) [A.M.]	60 min. walk [P.M.] or rest

Week 12 RECOVERY WEEK

	Swim	Cycle	Run
Monday	1250m [A.M.]	20km (12M) [P.M.]	—
Tuesday	1500m [A.M.]	—	20 min. [P.M.]
Wednesday	—	30km (18.5M) [A.M.]	—
Thursday	1500m [A.M.]	—	35 min. [P.M.]
Friday	—	30km (18.5M) [P.M.] or rest	—
Saturday	1000m [P.M.] or rest	—	50 min. [A.M.]
Sunday	—	60km (37M) [A.M.]	60 min. walk [P.M.] or rest

Week 13 SPEEDWORK/QUALITY PHASE

	Swim	Cycle	Run
Monday	1750m [A.M.]	40km (25M) [P.M.]	—
Tuesday	2000m [A.M.]	—	Quality [P.M.]
Wednesday	—	Quality [A.M.]	—
Thursday	Quality [A.M.]	—	30 min. [P.M.]
Friday	—	30km (18.5M) or rest	—
Saturday	1000m [P.M.] or rest	—	60 min. [A.M.]
Sunday	—	60km (37M) [A.M.]	60 min. walk [P.M.] or rest

Brick sessions

As you progress in triathlon, stringing disciplines together becomes vital to improving times. You can add a couple of 'brick' sessions to the speedwork/quality phase of this programme by including back-to-back bike-run sessions. Try this after your long ride on Sunday by simply adding a short 15–20-minute run after your cycle workout. Speed is not important. Simply experiencing the sensation of those bike-to-run jelly legs will prove invaluable on race day. Never do more than one 'brick' session a week.

Week 14 SPEEDWORK/QUALITY PHASE

	Swim	Cycle	Run
Monday	1750m [A.M.]	40km (25M) [P.M.]	—
Tuesday	2000m [A.M.]	—	Quality [P.M.]
Wednesday	—	Quality [A.M.]	—
Thursday	Quality [A.M.]	—	30 min. [P.M.]
Friday	—	30km (18.5M) [A.M.] or rest	—
Saturday	1000m [P.M.] or rest	—	60 min. [A.M.]
Sunday	—	60km (37M) [A.M.]	60 min. walk [P.M.] or rest

Week 16 SPEEDWORK/QUALITY PHASE

	Swim	Cycle	Run
Monday	1750m [A.M.]	40km (25M) [P.M.]	—
Tuesday	2000m [A.M.]	—	Quality [P.M.]
Wednesday	—	Quality [A.M.]	—
Thursday	Quality [A.M.]	—	30 min. [P.M.]
Friday	—	30km (18.5M) [A.M.] or rest	—
Saturday	1000m [P.M.] or rest	—	60 min. [A.M.]
Sunday	—	60km (37M) [A.M.]	60 min. walk [P.M.] or rest

Week 15 SPEEDWORK/QUALITY PHASE

	Swim	Cycle	Run
Monday	1750m [A.M.]	40km (25M) [P.M.]	—
Tuesday	2000m [A.M.]	—	Quality [P.M.]
Wednesday	—	Quality [A.M.]	—
Thursday	Quality [A.M.]	—	20 min. [P.M.]
Friday	—	30km (18.5M) [P.M.] or rest	—
Saturday	1000m [P.M.] or rest	—	60 min. [A.M.]
Sunday	—	60km (37M) [A.M.]	60 min. walk [P.M.] or rest

Week 17 BEGIN TAPER

	Swim	Cycle	Run
Monday	1500m [A.M.]	40km (25M) [P.M.]	—
Tuesday	2000m [A.M.]	—	30 min. [P.M.]
Wednesday	—	40km (25M) [A.M.]	—
Thursday	1000m [A.M.]	—	45 min. [P.M.]
Friday	Rest	Rest	Rest
Saturday	—	—	60 min. [A.M.]
Sunday	—	60km (37M) [A.M.]	45 min. walk [P.M.] or rest

Week 18 RACE WEEK

	Swim	Cycle	Run
Monday	1500m [A.M.]	40km (25M) [P.M.]	—
Tuesday	—	—	45 min. [A.M.]
Wednesday	1500m [A.M.]	40km (25M) [P.M.]	—
Thursday	Rest or travel	Rest or travel	Rest or travel
Friday	Rest	Rest	Rest
Saturday	RACE DAY		

Training Programmes

18 weeks (experienced): Half Ironman Distance

12 weeks (experienced): Ironman Distance

These two events separate the men from the boys (and the women from the girls)! This is tough, hardcore competition which can only be tackled if a triathlete has put in his or her requisite training and stayed the distance. The two training programmes are relatively long ones, but in making the step from Standard/Olympic to Half Ironman, triathletes are required to more than double their distances for both the cycling and running legs. In turn, the Ironman is exactly double in length to the Half Ironman for all three disciplines. You'll certainly be at your prime in terms of personal fitness and feeling good about yourself. Bear in mind that a crucial element at this level of competition is having the ability to apply a strong mental focus.

Dragon
5-6

PROGRAMME 6:

12 weeks (experienced)

by LouAnn Rivett – athlete, coach & physiotherapist

Ironman distance

3.9km swim, 180km cycle, 42.2km run
(2.4 miles; 112 miles; 26.2 miles)

The experts call it the 'toughest one-day event in the world'. Ironman winners are legends, and the finishers, heroes in their own right. There are many who have tried and many who have failed. The secret is in the training.
I have chosen a 12-week schedule for the Ironman. For many, it may seem too short a preparation time for an event of this magnitude, but I also believe that if training for an event is much longer than 12 weeks, it's extremely hard to maintain motivation. To find numerous Ironman programmes for a long build-up, visit this website – www.trinewbies.com – for some suggestions.

Am I ready?

You should have some triathlon experience. You need to comfortably swim 1km, cycle 60km and run 12km (0.5 mile; 37 miles; 7.5 miles), and you should be training regularly.

Training principles

- In an Ironman event, during both training and competing, mental strength counts for everything.
- Effective nutrition, vitamin supplementation and fluid replacement are crucial, as is adequate rest and sleep for recovery.
- Most of this programme is based on heart-rate percentages. If you don't know your heart rate, work out an effort level. Evidence shows that triathletes 'blow' during the run because their cycling heart rates are 10–20 beats too high at the start of the cycle.
- It is important to include gym sessions to develop core stability, which will affect your power output and speed in all three disciplines. See the Gym Routine pp43–45.

Week by week

- Include one rest day/easy day a week.
- Include one easy week every fourth week.
- The order and sequence of training sessions is important; do not switch sessions around.
- Keep to the heart-rate zones on long rides and runs.
- Don't increase time/mileage by more than 10–15%.
- Taper for the run, starting six weeks before the race.
- The Sunday swim is a recovery swim; go easy.

Cycling

Ensure that your bike setup is perfect. You will spend many hours on your bike so get it checked by a specialist to ensure a correct orthopaedic, neutral position that is comfortable and effective.

Swimming

No heart-rate percentages are given for the swim, since I believe that effective swimming training should be done in a squad under a coach. This will ensure correct technique and get the athlete used to swimming in a crowd.

Week 1

	Swim	Cycle/Gym	Run
Monday	Rest	Rest	Rest
Tuesday	30km (18.5M) 70%	—	8km (5M) 70%
Wednesday	1000m	Gym	—
Thursday	—	30km (18.5M) 70%	8km (5M) 70%
Friday	1000m	Gym	—
Saturday	1000m	60km (37M) 60–70%	—
Sunday	—	—	12km (7M) 60–70%

Week 2

	Swim	Cycle/Gym	Run
Monday	Rest	Rest	Rest
Tuesday	—	30km (18.5M) 70%	8km (5M) 70%
Wednesday	1500m	Gym	—
Thursday	—	30km 70%	8km (5M) 70%
Friday	1500m	Gym	—
Saturday	—	80km (50M) 60–70%	—
Sunday	1000m	—	15km (9M) 60–70%

Week 3

	Swim	Cycle/Gym	Run
Monday	Rest	Rest	Rest
Tuesday	—	30km (18.5M) 70%	8km (5M) 70%
Wednesday	2000m	Gym	—
Thursday	—	30km (18.5M) 80%	8km (5M) 70%
Friday	2000m	Gym	—
Saturday	—	100km (62M) 60–70%	—
Sunday	1000m	—	18km (11M) 60–70%

Week 4

	Swim	Cycle/Gym	Run
Monday	Rest	Rest	Rest
Tuesday	Rest	Rest	Rest
Wednesday	2000m	Gym	—
Thursday	—	20km (12M) 80%	8km (5M) 60–70%
Friday	2000m	—	—
Saturday	—	140km (87M) 70%	—
Sunday	1000m	—	25km (15.5M) 70%

Week 5

	Swim	Cycle/Gym	Run
Monday	Rest	Rest	Rest
Tuesday	—	20km (12M) 80%	8km (5M) 70%
Wednesday	2500m	Gym	—
Thursday	—	20km (12M) 70%	8km (5M) 75%
Friday	2500m	Gym	—
Saturday	—	140km (87M) 70%	—
Sunday	1000m	—	25km (15.5M) 70%

Week 6

	Swim	Cycle/Gym	Run
Monday	Rest	Rest	Rest
Tuesday	—	40km (25M) 80%	8km (5M) 70%
Wednesday	3000m	Gym	—
Thursday	—	40km (25M) 70%	6km (4M) 80%
Friday	3000m	Gym	—
Saturday	—	100km (62M) 70%	—
Sunday	1000m	—	32km (20M) 70%

Week 7

	Swim	Cycle/Gym	Run
Monday	Rest	Rest	Rest
Tuesday	—	20km (12M) 80%	8km (5M) 70%
Wednesday	3500m	Gym	—
Thursday	—	30km (18.5M) 70%	12km (7M) 80%
Friday	3500m	Gym	—
Saturday	—	160km (99M) 60%	—
Sunday	1000m	—	21km (13M) 70%

Week 8

RECOVERY WEEK

	Swim	Cycle/Gym	Run
Monday	Rest	Rest	Rest
Tuesday	Rest	Rest	Rest
Wednesday	3000m	Gym	—
Thursday	—	20km (12M) 70%	10km (6M) 80%
Friday	3000m	—	6km (4M) 60%
Saturday	—	180km (112M) 70%	—
Sunday	1000m	—	24km (15M) 70%

Week 9

	Swim	Cycle/Gym	Run
Monday	Rest	Rest	Rest
Tuesday	—	30km (18.5M) 90%	10km (6M) 60–70%
Wednesday	4000m	Gym	—
Thursday	—	30km (18.5M) 60–70%	12km (7M) 85%
Friday	2000m	Gym	—
Saturday	—	140km (87M) 70%	—
Sunday	1000m	—	21km (13M) 70%

Week 10

TAPER

	Swim	Cycle	Run
Monday	Rest	Rest	Rest
Tuesday	—	40km (25M) 90%	10km (6M) 60–70%
Wednesday	4000m	Gym	—
Thursday	—	30km (18.5M) 70%	12km (7M) 90%
Friday	2000m	Gym	—
Saturday	—	100km (62M) 70%	—
Sunday	1000m	—	15km (9M) 70%

Week 11

TAPER

	Swim	Cycle/Gym	Run
Monday	Rest	Rest	Rest
Tuesday	—	40km (25M) 70%	10km (6M) 80%
Wednesday	3000m	Gym	—
Thursday	—	40km (25M) 80%	12km (7M) 60–70%
Friday	3000m	—	—
Saturday	—	50km (30M) 70%	—
Sunday	—	—	12km (7M) 60–70%

Week 12

	Swim	Cycle/Gym	Run
Monday	Rest	Rest	Rest
Tuesday	Rest	Rest	Rest
Wednesday	800m	10km (6M)	—
Thursday	Rest	Rest	Rest
Friday	—	—	3km (2M)
Saturday	RACE DAY		

What the elite do

During peak training, athletes pushing for a top-three finish will swim 20–25km, cycle 650–700km and run 70–80km a week (12–15.5 miles; 405–435 miles; 43.5–50 miles). Their longest run will be 42km (26.2 miles), six weeks prior to the event.

CONRAD STOLTZ

Q&A with an off-road champion

One of the newest and potentially most thrilling forms of triathlon is the off-road format.

As a direct result of the Xterra series in the USA, off-road triathlon has spawned an exciting new breed of triathletes able to negotiate tough swims, technical mountain bike trails and cross-country running. Presently top of the list of off-road triathletes is South African Conrad Stoltz, the 2001 World Xterra champion and former Olympian who, in the same year, won every off-road triathlon he participated in.

Q: How does off-road triathlon differ from traditional road triathlon?

A: Xterra is such a new sport (especially to me and my coach) that I think we are only scratching the surface of what training for such a demanding event entails. Obviously the mountain biking skills are the most important to learn. I have seen world-class triathletes lose as much as 25 minutes on the bike. It takes lots of skill, but also a strong nerve, concentration and experience.

Equipment also plays a big role. Tyre selection, tyre pressure and suspension setup are just a few aspects that can make or break your race.

Q: How easy is it to hone the technical skills needed in off-road triathlon?

A: You can practise your skills to a large extent, but good genes will make a champion. I raced BMX as a kid and rode off-road bikes since I was eight years old, so developed my skills early.

Since focusing on Xterra, I spent a lot of time in the off-season working on my skills. For two months I only cycled off-road, practising skills with downhill specialists, playing around with setup, equipment, techniques and terrains. I did a few low-key races too.

During serious training I took chances I wouldn't take in-season, and I crashed a lot – although nothing serious! Gary Mandy, my Xterra training partner has a good quote: 'A ride is not a ride until there is blood'.

Once serious training starts, I only go off-road once every week or two. I practise technique only – not trying to gain fitness. I look for a technical section, go over it very slowly with a friend, pick the lines and then set out to ride them, starting slow and picking up the speed as I learn how to ride the new obstacles and my confidence grows.

Q: Other than bike skills, what else has changed since you began off-road triathlon?

A: Apart from the technical training I haven't changed my training much, as I still race nondrafting on the road and also have my eye on the Athens Olympics in 2004 (where the swimming is very important).

There will be a time when off-road triathlons will be so competitive that I shall have to focus on that. I could get away with much less swimming (from the 25km [15.5 miles] a week I'm doing now to probably 15km [9 miles]) and concentrate much more on the bike and the run.

5 NUTRITION IN TRIATHLON

What you put in is what you get out. Yes, it's a cliché, but in the sport of triathlon this is a cliché you'll do well to heed. Unlike single-sport activities, the nature of triathlon means that nutrition, hydration and supplementation become critical to success. During hard training a triathlete will sometimes do three different training sessions a day, and the effects on the overall health of the body are enormous. Body fatigue, reduced immunity and an unhealthy lack of body fat are common among triathletes who sometimes train too hard while ignoring their increased nutritional needs. The result is sickness, injury and a lack of performance.

For a triathlete, the key to sound nutritional intake is to be aware of the effects training has on the body. If, as a triathlete in training, you are stroking out a 3000m swim in the morning, then following up with a lunchtime and later an evening workout, there is little doubt that the answer to good recovery and continued sickness-free training is the consumption of sufficient carbohydrates, vitamins and minerals. So, first you need to look at the various components of good nutrition.

What is a good diet? In this chapter you will be able to get an idea of how to construct a good eating plan – but there is no exact formula. Everyone has different tastes, different nutritional needs and different budgets – so you need to settle for a balanced diet that you can maintain.

As with any diet, your choice of what you eat needs to be sustainable. Many of these get-thin-quick fad diets work in the short term but are difficult to maintain as a lifestyle change.

If your diet needs a major overhaul, make changes slowly since a radical change is difficult to manage. Take a month to make subtle variations – the disruption will be minimal and the results sustainable. In this chapter, you will also be introduced to pre- and post-race nutrition, probably two of the least understood areas of nutrition. Correctly done, eating right can be as beneficial as training right.

DIET

The body relies on three basic dietary components to keep it healthy and fit.

Carbohydrates

In the world of endurance sport, carbohydrates are essential. Once they are ingested, they are turned into glucose and stored in the muscles and liver as glycogen – from where they provide a fast source of energy for the body. There are three types of carbohydrates: slow-, intermediate- and quick-digesting. Each type has benefits for the triathlete – for day-to-day eating the slow and intermediate carbohydrates are preferable to those that are digested fast, while quick-digesting carbs are more beneficial during an ultradistance race when quick energy, and not a full stomach, is needed.

Protein

Protein is muscle food. Without adequate protein from foods such as red meat (also an excellent source of iron) and lean chicken – and for vegetarians eggs, cheese and legumes – muscles damaged through training don't rebuild adequately, and recovery and strength are compromised. It is unfortunate, though, that a lot of protein foods come with fat as a byproduct.

Fats

For many triathletes, this is the swearword of nutrition. However, ultimately it is the kind of fat you eat that is important. The trick is to avoid 'bad' (saturated) fats – such as fried chips, sausages and cheddar cheese – and concentrate on taking in 'good' (mono- and polyunsaturated) fats – such as that from avocadoes, olives, olive oil and sunflower seeds. Nuts such as almonds, walnuts and cashews are also a good source.

Eating before and after a race

Prerace meals

If triathletes were simply cyclists, you could probably take in a fairly sizable breakfast on the morning of the race, but once you plan to lie horizontal in the water for a swim, the last thing you need is a heavy belly and heartburn. What to do?

The key to prerace nutrition is to find out what works for you as an individual. Never try something new on race day. Practise with different options beforehand during your training – both the night before and on the morning of the training session. You need to ensure you have the least disruption from high-bulk foods on race day.

Recommended by *Runner's World* (South Africa) nutritionist Jane Downs the day before a race:

- Breakfast

Oats with ½ cup low-fat milk or low-fat yoghurt.

- Lunch and supper

Pasta with a tomato and onion sauce, with slices of lean beef, chicken or ham. (It is better to avoid dairy-based filled pastas and sauces, as milk is a common allergen – milk intolerance could cause diarrhoea or irritable bowel syndrome.)

- Fruit

Drink pure juices but avoid the pulp or pieces of fruit, as they are high in fibre.

- Carbohydrate drinks

Choose drinks high in glucose polymers which are more slowly broken down, and therefore a better source of long-lasting energy. (It is best to go for glucose polymers in foil packaging; they are better preserved this way. If kept in clear packaging and exposed to sunlight, they only become sweet.)

- High-fibre foods

Avoid any beans (pulses), bran muffins, wholewheat or brown bread and other high-fibre foods as they promote bowel movement. Not good for race day!

For the prerace meal, it is better to opt for intermediate digesting products like energy ('power') bars or baby potatoes/basmati rice. Eat at least two hours before you race to make sure the carbohydrates have been fully digested.

6 RACE DAY

You're finally there: goggles sitting neatly on your forehead, bike racked in transition, your body a mass of twitching nervous energy. Even if it isn't cold, you feel cold; your legs feel weakened and you question your ability and training. Around you are some of the fittest individuals, each a master of three disciplines and each with his or her own performance agenda for the day. They come in all shapes and sizes: some are lithe and lean, muscular bodies taut and legs shaved, but most will be no different from any other sport event. Some are overweight, others quite happy with unshaven legs – and some look plain unsuited to this multi-disciplined sport. The lean and mean will have their day upfront, while the majority will be up against themselves, pushing their bodies to limits they never imagined before.

It truly is an exhilarating feeling standing at the start of a triathlon. You should remember, though, that preparation is everything. A triathlete needs to double-check everything from cycling helmet to water bottles to running shoes.

WHAT TO EXPECT

No matter who you are, how hard you've trained or how many triathlons you've done previously, every triathlete is nervous at the start line. Don't fool yourself when you look around and wonder why so many seem so relaxed – each triathlete has his own way of coping with nervous energy. Some joke and banter with their friends, while others prefer solitude, to focus on the task ahead.

Before a triathlon, the transition zone is a hive of activity. Those who get there early take up the prime positions on the bike racks (so that the bike is closest to the mount line) while the rest jockey for position to find an easy exit and comfortable place to sit. The size of the triathlon event plays a large part in deciding how early to set yourself up. I give myself at least an hour before the start of even a short-course race – once you've registered, paid your entry fee, got your swim stuff, cycle and running gear together, and set up a transition zone, there's not much time for a warm-up if you arrive any later.

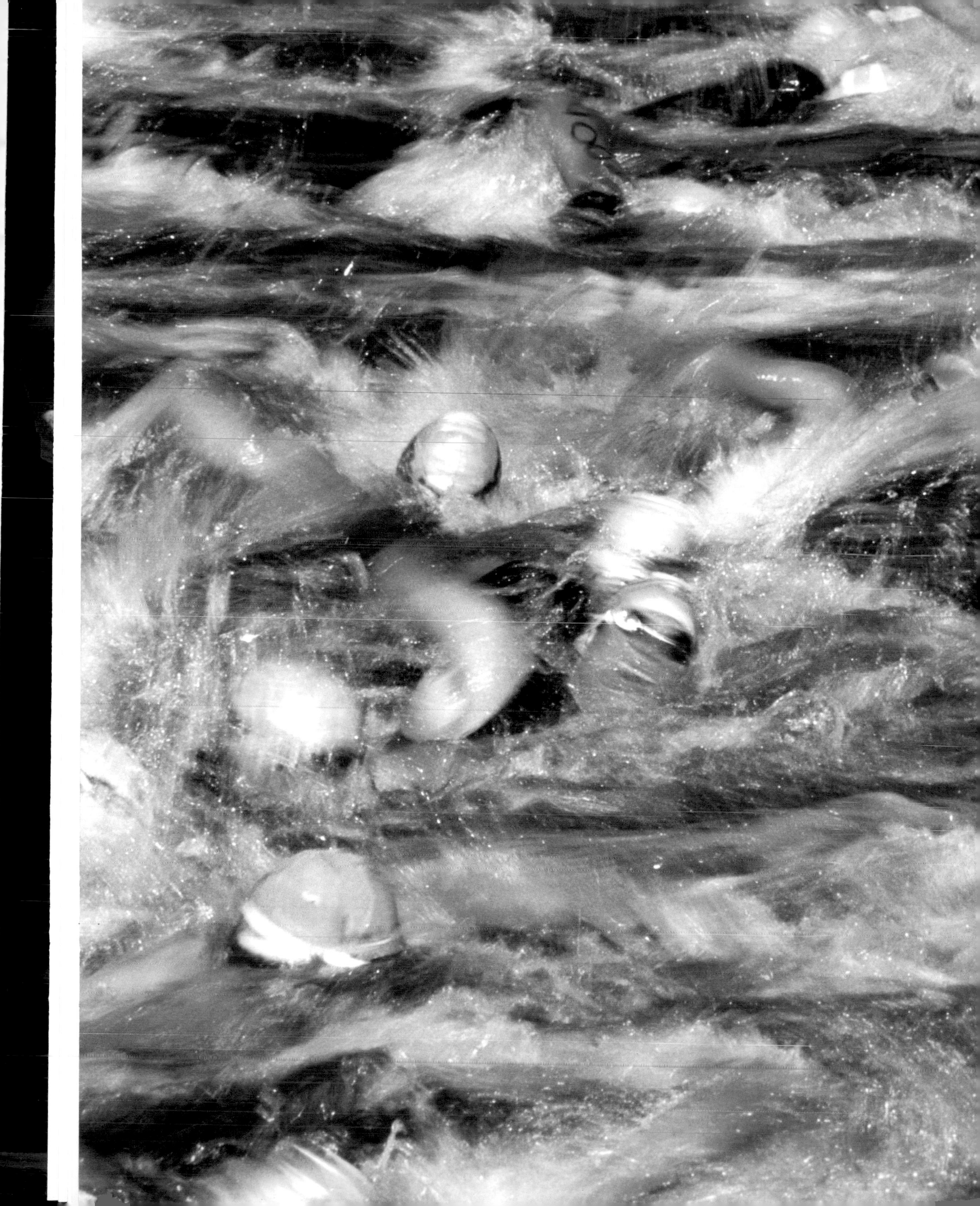

Transitions

What to expect

In-between all of the action there are the transitions, the focus of every race. Elite triathletes can be in and out of T1 (the swim-bike transition) and T2 (the bike-run transition) under 20 seconds, while others can take a couple of minutes. For the novice, quick transitions are not as important as for the more experienced, but whatever your ability, the lure of 'free time' – in other words, time that can be made up just by practising simple transition techniques – should never be passed up.

During the swim-to-bike phase the transition area is a hive of activity, bustling with chaotic energy as athletes strip off wetsuits, scramble for shoes and helmets and dash towards the mount line. Simply finding your bike can be hard, as you'll be disoriented from the swim. If you're wearing a wetsuit, it'll feel like a straitjacket as it sticks to your body so start removing the arms and upper body section as soon as you exit the water. Once it's off, getting your cycling top on is just as sticky, as wet bodies and Lycra are not the best of friends.

During the bike-to-run leg, the field will have spread out so there is less chaos but more fatigue. Athletes often take longer as they use the transition area to gather their thoughts and focus on the run section ahead.

For the triathlete who has practised his transition changes during training, it is an opportunity to gain seconds over rivals and shave off that little extra for a personal best.

Ultra tip

In long-distance events, instead of eating in transition, tape food to your bike so you can eat while you ride. You can use masking tape to attach food to your centre bar as it is easy to split and break.

How to handle it

Be prepared

Lay all your equipment on a towel, cycling equipment first, then running shoes, and so on. Place everything as neatly as possible and as close to your own bike as you can, so that athletes finishing ahead of you don't knock your equipment to all parts of the transition area.

Water and a seat

Some triathletes keep a bowl of fresh water and a small stool in transition to get rid of any sand (there's nothing worse!) before they put on their cycling shoes. A low stool is also handy to sit on while changing and makes it easier to get up once you're ready.

Clip in

The simplest swim-to-bike technique is to clip your cycling shoes in the pedals before the start of the race. Make sure the shoes are loose and easy to slide into. Slide on helmet and sunglasses, and head for the mount line. When you first start pedalling, place your feet on top of the shoes, slipping them in once you have momentum on a flat or downhill. Remember that the time-saving element is not about how fast you put your feet into the shoes but how quickly you start pedalling.

Powder them

If you're not wearing socks, sprinkle your cycling shoes with talcum powder to help slide your wet feet in.

Bike-to-run transitions

To ensure a fast transition, practise pulling your feet out of your cycling shoes before you reach the dismount line. Ride with your feet on top of your shoes, then as you get closer to the change, swing one leg over the bike and dismount as you slow down. This takes some practice so *never* try it in a race if you haven't mastered it in training.

OVERTRAINING

A common ailment in triathlon, overtraining is simple in theory: this is when exercise outpaces your recovery period and the body is unable to adapt. In practice, it is a lot harder to guard against. Overtraining manifests itself in many forms, but one of the most common symptoms is mood swings. An exhausted athlete will often become depressed and irritable, and rapidly become demotivated, sick and can even suffer sleep disorders. In women, overtraining can interfere with their menstrual cycle.

It is vital that anyone training for an event as gruelling as a triathlon constantly monitors his or her training, ensuring that the build-up is slow and steady with plenty of recovery and rest. The best way to do this is to monitor your daily resting heart rate – since your sympathetic nervous system plays a part in how your body responds to stress, through heart rate, blood pressure and the body's energy reserves. Either take a manual measurement (place your middle finger on the underside of your wrist and count the number of beats for 10 seconds, then multiply by six) or use a heart-rate monitor to check your resting pulse before you get out of bed in the morning. If the rate is 10 beats or more higher than normal on any given day, you may be putting in too much – or you are ill. Either way, it's time to take a break.

If you find that training has gone from being the highlight of your day to being a constant drudge, you may be overdoing it. Note that knowing whether you're simply suffering from an 'off day' as opposed to training too hard comes with experience, but it's crucial to success.

The treatment is logical: take time off. Rest your body until you find that desire to train again. When you do start, begin slowly so that you constantly feel ready to do more. Initially you should finish each session feeling as if you could do it all over again. That way you'll remain motivated while also allowing your body to physically recover. Remember: you can never train too easily, but you can often train too hard.

Swimmer's ear

A pool filled with other swimmers is a breeding ground for many forms of bacteria. Everyone has bacteria in the ear canal, but the moist, alkaline environment can cause a painful and itchy infection and inflammation in the outer ear canal which may lead to a full-blown ear infection.

In extreme cases, an entire swimming squad could pick up an infection – which is more the result of a poorly sanitized pool than individual susceptibility to ear infection. Take the matter up with the people who run the pool.

Treatment

The best form of treatment is preventive. After every swim, shake your head to one side, then the other to rid your ears of any excess water, then use a clean towel to dry out the inside of the ear. It's simple and effective.

You can also buy over-the-counter eardrops containing an antiseptic. If you're prone to ear infections it's probably wise to wear a waterproof swimcap over the ears and use the drops both before and after a swim. Avoid earplugs, since these can trap infection inside the ear!

You can prepare your own eardrops from a combination of half vinegar and half hydrogen peroxide, although this solution has a shelf life of only a week. You can also use vinegar on its own; it restores the acidity of the ear. Buy an empty glass bottle with a short, stubby nozzle, sterilize it in boiling water and use for storing the mixture. These solutions should only be preventive measures and should not be used to treat swimmer's ear.

In severe cases where there is some kind of discharge, it is best to consult your doctor since a serious infection can have a consequence on your health.

Swimmer's eye (conjunctivitis)

Swimmer's eye is a common complaint among swimmers who wear ill-fitting goggles or none at all. It is often caused by chlorine irritation or anti-fogging agents used in goggles, and leaves the eyes itchy and scratchy.

Treatment

Try over-the-counter eye drops or visit a doctor for a diagnosis. Get yourself a pair of goggles that fit properly!

Swimming-leg 'whack'

Although not an inherent cause of swimming itself, triathletes may receive a 'whack' at the start of the swim leg. Arms swing, legs thrash and feet kick in the fight for clear water. Almost every triathlon swimmer will inevitably have experienced the painful whack of an arm or a foot during that first portion of a triathlon swim.

Treatment

So you got a kick in the face, your goggles were knocked off and you're feeling dazed and short of breath. Assess how badly you've been hurt: if you feel swelling, you're probably sporting a nice shiner. If you're failing to recover quickly and you're feeling dazed and panicky, then it's time for drastic measures. If you simply can't continue, try to pull to the side of the swimming pack and raise your arm to notify one of the rescue crew that you need help. Depending on the severity of your injury, anything from an ice pack to stitches will be necessary. The best treatment, of course, is prevention!

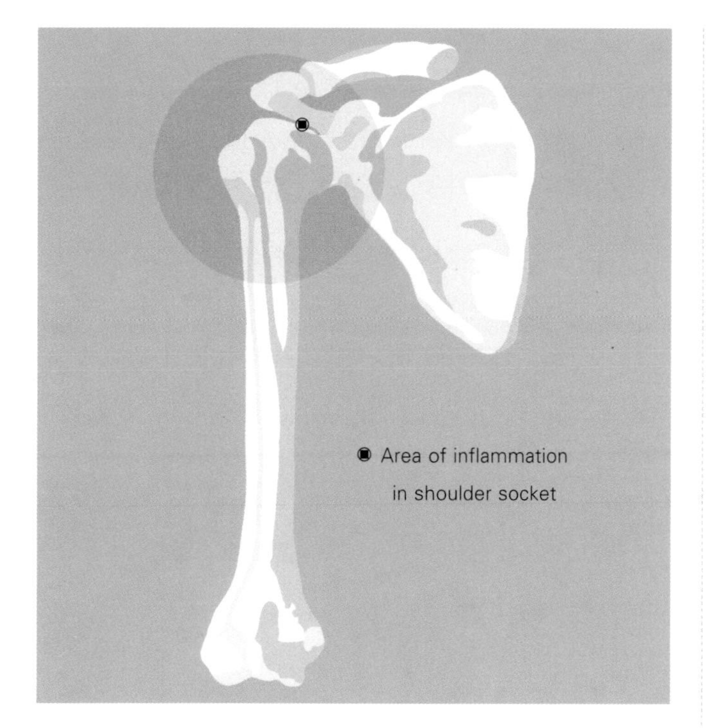

Swimmer's shoulder

This is probably the most common of swimming injuries. Due to the repetitive nature of swimming (the shoulder rotates around 1300 times for every 1.5km, or mile, swum in freestyle), the 17 different muscles that hold the humerus (the upper arm, from shoulder to elbow) in the shoulder socket can become inflamed. The joint becomes unstable, and tendons become inflamed and are pinched or impinged upon, which can be chronically painful. For swimmers who have had this complaint (I being one of them!), it can be one of the most debilitating injuries.

Treatment

As with all injuries, prevention is better than cure. Top international swimming coach Terry Laughlin recommends a four-step plan:

- Warm-up

Follow five to 10 minutes of gentle swimming with the exercises below. Do two repetitions each at 10–30 seconds per rep before and after your swim workout.

- For the muscles underneath the shoulder

Extend both arms overhead in the streamlined position, then from the waist lean first to the left side as far as possible, then to the right. Feel the pull all the way down your side.

- For the muscles in front of the shoulder

Extend both arms straight behind your back, fingers interlaced and slowly, steadily, raise your arms up behind you as far as possible.

- The muscles in the back of the shoulder

Extend one arm across your chest so that the shoulder is under your chin and the hand, forearm and upper arm are parallel to the ground. Without turning your body, use your other hand to pull the arm as close to your chest as possible. Alternate with the other arm.

If you do end up with swimmer's shoulder, the first step is to reduce the inflammation by applying an ice pack (a bag of frozen peas is ideal). Also, take a low dose of aspirin or ibuprofen. A physiotherapist may use ultrasound therapy to speed up healing.

Only in severe cases will a doctor use a cortisone treatment (which can lead to tendon rupture) or even surgery. The trick is never to get to that point.

Cyclists are always telling runners that cycling is an injury-free sport. They're wrong. No matter what sport you take part in, if you do too much and don't recover properly, injury in even the 'safest' sports is inevitable.

Cycling injuries are most often caused by setting up your bike poorly, particularly in terms of sore, stiff shoulders, and lower back and knee pain. So the first port of call for any novice cyclist should be the local cycle shop, for help in setting up the bike accurately.

'Numb nuts'

Whether it's numbness between you and the seat or a condition of the hands known as 'cyclist's palsy', numb body parts is a common problem in cycling. Studies have shown that the pressure put on the perineum (the area you sit on) can make men impotent if allowed to continue for large periods of time (professional cyclists are at high risk). Cyclist's palsy is a condition where the hands become numb from compressing the ulnar nerve at the base of your wrists while riding. This is dangerous as you lose the feel of the handlebars.

Treatment

There are a number of ways to take the pressure off the perineum:

Buy a custom seat

Many modern cycling seat manufacturers have developed seats specifically made for men and women. If you battle with this complaint, it's a worthwhile investment in personal comfort.

Get strong

Novice cyclists tend to suffer more than experienced cyclists because they don't generate as much lifting power in their legs and tend to sit harder on the saddle. The stronger you become as a cyclist, the less you'll suffer.

Vary your stance

Top professional cyclists can ride for up to eight hours without pain purely because they vary their stance between sitting and standing, alleviating pressure on the perineum. During training, practise standing even when you're cycling on the flats. Not only does it alleviate numbness but it'll also help stretch your back.

If you're suffering from cyclist's palsy, invest in a pair of properly padded cycling gloves and add an extra roll of handlebar tape to the bars. You should also vary your hand position regularly and don't grip the handlebars too tightly – a relaxed but firm grip is all you need.

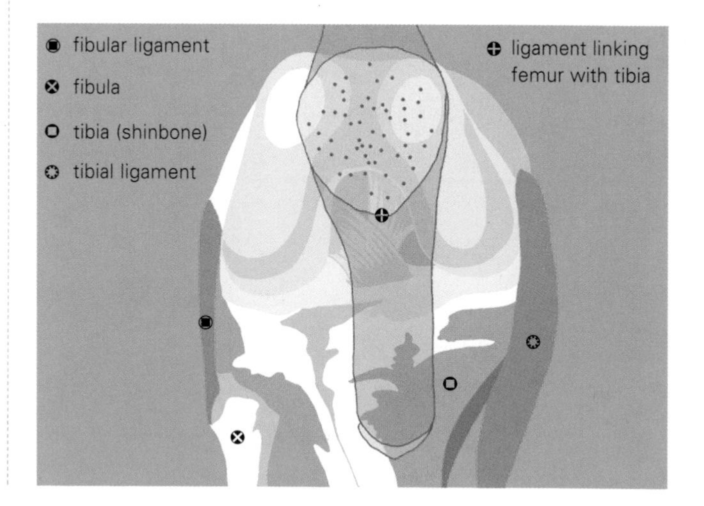

Cyclist's knee

The knee is a complex hinge joint between the femur (thighbone), tibia (shinbone) and patella (kneecap). A fibrous joint capsule encases these three bones, allowing some rotation, and forward/backward movement. It is this joint that causes problems for cyclists and runners. Pain is normally felt underneath or to the side of the kneecap and is usually the result of misalignment in the knees and feet, and/or too much high-resistance training, which can damage and weaken the delicate ligaments around the knee.

Also, a saddle that is set too low means that the knee is constantly flexed through the pedal stroke, putting strain on the ligaments. On the other hand, if the saddle is too high, back and hip problems may occur. Knee pain is normally gradual, starting with a slight ache but later developing into a 'hobbling' injury that leaves you battling to walk normally.

Treatment

To rule out a poor bike fit, consult p28 on bike setup or have your seat position checked. The second focus should be to correct any biomechanical difficulties; a biomechanist or specialized podiatrist can advise you. The way you train should also be considered. Limit your strength training to once a week. When cycling, try to maintain a high cadence of between 80 and 90 rpm; good pedal speed is not only about injury-prevention – it is also the most efficient method of pedalling. You can use shorter cranks on your bike, too, which improves pedal speed, thus limiting pressure applied to the tendons when pushing a high gear.

Unfortunately, rest is the only treatment for cyclist's knee, although mild anti-inflammatories and ice therapy can reduce swelling in the area.

'Hot foot'

Cycling shoes, unlike those for running, are stiff, unforgiving items that offer little shock absorption from hard road surfaces and they are often narrow and constricting – but the benefits of support and power transfer outweigh the use of running shoes as a viable alternative. As a result, cyclists often suffer from a condition known as 'hot foot', caused by excessive pressure on the balls of the feet during hard effort. Cyclists with biomechanical problems, such as high arches or excessive pronation, suffer more than those with neutral feet.

Treatment

Insert a padded sock liner into the shoes to help protect against road vibration. Also ensure that your cleat position is correct (the ball of your foot should be on the centre of the pedal). Give your feet a bit of breathing room by loosening the straps on your shoes – remember that your feet swell the hotter they get, so make allowances as you ride.

For chronic problems, you should see a biomechanist or podiatrist about custom-made orthotics. With orthotics, your feet don't absorb all the vibratory energy, helping you transfer more power to the pedal.

Back pain

As cyclists become fatigued, they lose core abdominal strength around the lower half of the torso, which stresses the muscles here, resulting in pain and stiffness. Bad posture and poor bike setup is the culprit. In severe cases, the lower back muscles become so weak that the spine is actually forced to carry the load. Here, degeneration of the spine can occur.

Treatment

First of all, ensure that your bike setup is correct (see p28). If the distance between the saddle and the stem of the handlebars is either too far or too close, the back is either overextended or cramped. It's also vital that cyclists do regular active stretching (see pp60–61) to strengthen the lower back muscles and improve their range of motion.

The best way to check your posture on the bike is to stand up straight, then bend your body forward from the hips, keeping your back straight. This is the position you need to maintain on the bike. Try to push your navel towards the horizontal top tube; this will help bring your hips forward and flatten out the lower half of your back. It will also help to reduce neck pain, as the angle of the neck at the top of the torso is flatter.

In severe cases of lower back pain, a doctor can prescribe anti-inflammatory medication and muscle relaxants, although it's best not to numb pain. Pain is something that should be monitored and not disguised by drugs.

You can also use an ice pack to reduce swelling, but follow it with a moist heat pack to help blood flow within the area. Massage is another alternative that can do wonders for lower back problems.

Road rash

If a cyclist falls onto a hard road surface, friction against the skin shreds off the top layers of the epidermis and the deeper dermis. The deeper the abrasion, the more blood – although even a mild skin abrasion is painful. Without proper treatment, abrasions can become infected.

Treatment

The simplest way to treat road rash used to be clean soap and water, an antiseptic cream and a dressing. But new research suggests that this method may not be ideal since it can further damage the injured area, making healing slower. Some antiseptics actually harm the tissue and affect the regeneration of cells within the wound. The best method is to clean the area using sterile water under pressure (a syringe is ideal). You can even use gauze to lightly clean the area, but don't rub hard or you'll do more damage. After the wound is cleaned, cover the area with a dressing. Change the dressing regularly, keeping the area moist – it heals quicker, protecting itself against infection.

It is also advisable to guard against tetanus (an infectious disease that affects muscles) if the wound is open. If the abrasion is full of deep cuts, then see a doctor as stitches may be needed.

Head injuries

Almost 80% of cyclists who die in accidents suffer some sort of head trauma. Many are those cyclists who take on the Tour de France without wearing a helmet – and they pay the ultimate price. Head injuries are serious, and should never be self-treated.

Treatment

Prevention is better than cure so *always wear a helmet*. No matter where you ride, ensure that you do not fail to wear a proper-fitting helmet.

If you do have a fall and your helmet is struck, replace it immediately – even if it looks like there is no damage. Often a damaged helmet will appear fine when in actual fact its shock-absorbing qualities have been compromised.

If you're involved in a serious crash and you suffer concussion, make sure you get to a doctor as soon as possible to check for skull fractures or internal bleeding. Often these injuries fail to show up early, only to have fatal consequences later.

If you witness an accident involving possible head injuries, avoid removing the patient's helmet and moving him or her. Wait for expert medical attention. If the patient is unconscious, assume that there has been a neck injury until proven otherwise.

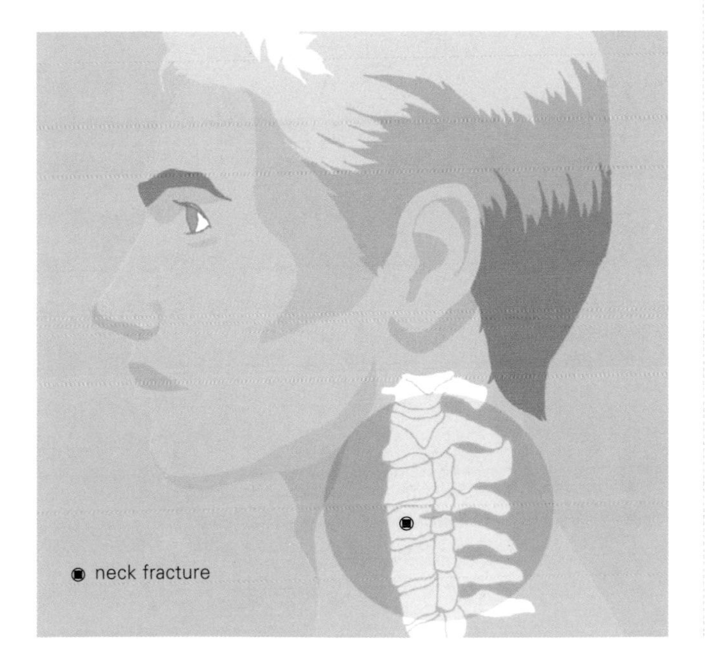

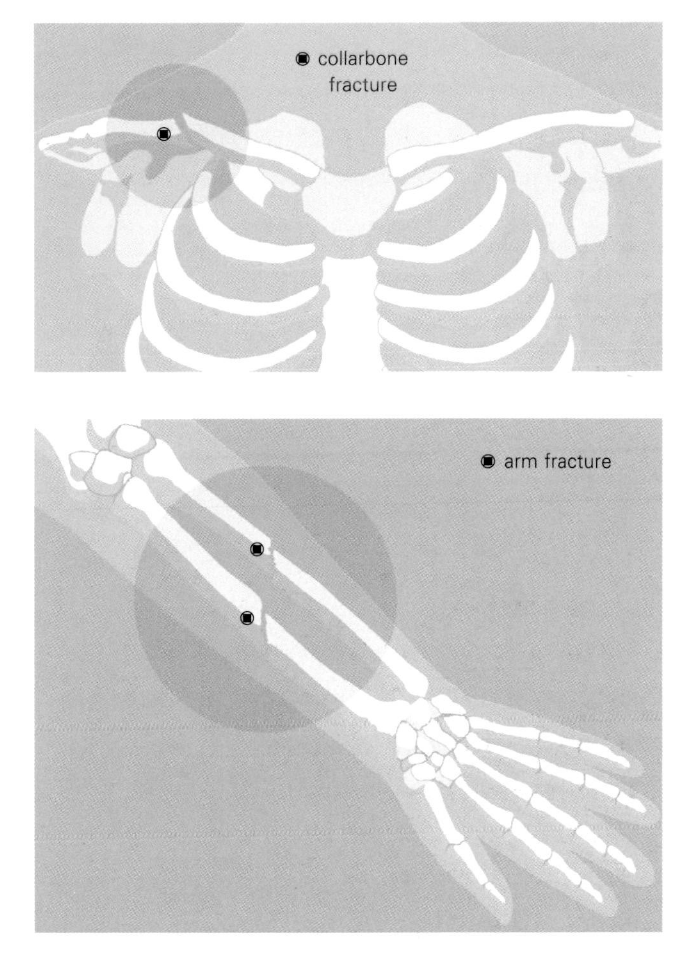

Fractures

In cyclists, fractures of the collarbone (the result of the classic 'over the handlebars' fall) and ribs are the most common. A fracture of the ribs can sometimes result in a punctured lung, so, after a hard fall, always check for any breathing difficulties or bruising around the rib cage.

Treatment

In the event of a suspected broken bone of any kind, immobilize the affected area and seek medical treatment as soon as possible.

Because of its high impact, running is often maligned as being the sport most likely to cause injury. However, almost all injuries are caused by poor training build-up and running too often, too soon. It is among novice runners that injuries mostly occur, simply because they fail to strengthen the muscles, tendons and ligaments enough to cope with high mileage and more speed. When novices first start running, there is rapid development of the cardiovascular system which makes runners believe they are capable of going faster and further. Unfortunately, muscles, ligaments and tendons take longer to adapt – and injury occurs. In more experienced runners, a lack of adequate recovery is normally the culprit.

While triathletes have the advantage of being able to cross train, they, too, still have their fair share of running ailments. If you suffer regularly from running-related injuries, check that you're wearing the correct shoes (see p34–35). It is important to match running shoes to foot type – only then can you isolate training as a possible cause. Once this has been established and the pain still persists, you should consult a sports physician or sports physiotherapist.

Stitches

Whether you've run 10 marathons or have just started a running career, stitches can affect anyone. It's a condition so common that there are very few who have never experienced it.

Normally a stitch is felt on the underside of the rib cage when bouncing movements cause your stomach to pull on the ligaments that attach your stomach to your diaphragm. This can cause pain so severe that it often brings runners to a complete standstill.

Recent research in New Zealand suggests that the most effective way to prevent a stitch is to support the stomach. The best way to do that is to focus on keeping your stomach muscles tight, especially on downhills where bouncing increases. Also, try to avoid drinking too much before a race or during the bike leg. The more fluid in your stomach, the heavier it becomes and the harder the tugging on the diaphragm ligaments.

If you do develop a stitch, breathe out with pursed lips; this helps contract your stomach muscles. You can also apply pressure with your fingers on the painful area, supporting it and limiting the bounce.

The best preventive measure is to teach yourself to belly breathe. This involves pushing out the stomach (not only expanding your upper lungs) when breathing in, and pulling in the stomach when breathing out. This encourages the diaphragm to expand fully during the breathing process.

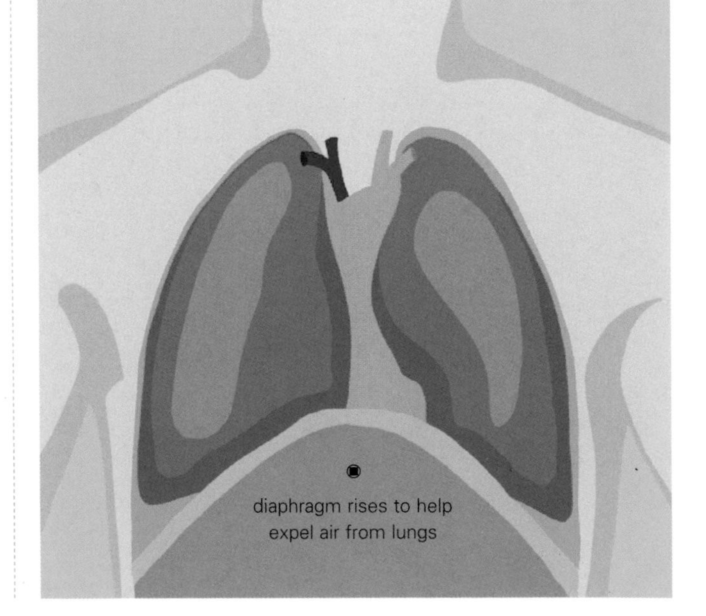

Chondromalacia

This is also known as 'runner's knee' and is the name given to an achy, sandpapery knee condition. Poor tracking of the kneecap, which in turn softens and breaks down the cartilage behind the kneecap causing pain, is one of the major causes. You can often diagnose chondromalacia by putting your hand on your knee and bending it; the kneecap will grind as the rough cartilage rubs inside the joint.

Initial symptoms are nagging pain on the underside of the kneecap, but the pain can be severe if left untreated.

Treatment

Ease off on running time and ice the area with an ice pack three to four times a day (15–20 minutes at a time); then massage the sore spots around the knee (the short-term solution). The long-term goal is to strengthen the quadriceps that control the tracking of the kneecap. You can either do a series of short leg presses with your feet facing out; or do a series of step-ups onto an elevated surface. The important part of these step-ups is to do them sideways and very slowly. The step should be about a foot off the ground. Do 40 step-ups on each leg, every two days.

Iliotibial Band Syndrome (ITBS)

ITBS starts as a dull pain on the outside of the knee but quickly becomes painful, even to the point where the athlete can't walk. It happened to me in 1994 during a long-distance triathlon. I had two hours to finish the last 8km (5 miles) to hit my goal time, when my niggling ITB (iliotibial band) injury struck with a vengeance. At first I was forced to walk the downhills, but I conceded after I struggled to walk at all! The injury is caused by the iliotibial band rubbing against the femur on the outside of the knee. The friction causes irritation and inflammation, and occurs when there's a shortening of the IT band caused by anything from bowlegs, overpronation and too many downhill workouts to too much sprintwork.

Treatment

First ensure that your shoes aren't worn, as this is a common cause. Second, look at your training: did you do too many fast sessions or suddenly increase your mileage?

Ice three to four times a day for 20 minutes. Massage the area using circular motions, and stretch regularly. If the problem persists, see a biomechanist to check if you need an orthotic to correct any biomechanical problems.

The rocking stretch is the most effective for ITB. Lie on your back with your knees bent, feet on the floor. Place your right ankle on top of your left knee, link your hands around the front of the left leg and pull the leg towards your chest to stretch the side of the right leg and into the glutes; hold for 30–40 seconds to relax and lengthen the muscle. Do three times to each side, three times a day.

Shin splints

This is often better referred to as tendonitis of the lower leg, since it involves inflammation of the muscles and tendons around the shins – the front of the lower leg. It is common in triathletes, as they often run on tired legs when tendons tend to take the strain usually handled by the muscles. Novice runners or runners training again after a long lay-off are most susceptible to shin splints.

The onset of pain is gradual, starting with an aching pain down both sides of the shinbone. In severe cases it can develop into stress fractures of the bone. Pronation problems can also be a cause, as can running on hard, unforgiving surfaces.

Treatment

Unlike injuries such as ITBS, you can run through a mild case of the shin splints. Mild pain is often part of the legs' adaptation process – it can be tolerated during early season training, when your muscles are readapting to the increased load on them.

The key, though, is to know when you should rest to prevent the injury from worsening. The best test is running itself: if the leg feels better after it's warmed up, then continue with light training. However, if the injury gets worse as you run, it's far better to rest or seek professional help. Physiotherapists sometimes use ultrasound therapy to speed up recovery.

As with most leg injuries, ice therapy works to control inflammation; place an ice pack or a bag of frozen peas on the area for 15–20 minutes three to four times a day. Low doses of aspirin or ibuprofen also help.

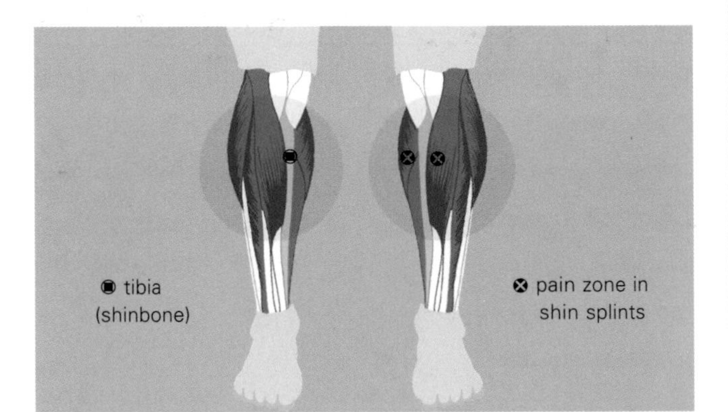

Hamstring tears

Although there are occasions when a triathlete can suffer from an acute or sudden hamstring tear, most hamstring injuries start gradually and get steadily worse. Since the hamstring is one of the largest muscle groups in the human body, a chronic hamstring tear can be among the most debilitating of injuries.

When the tear is chronic, it is difficult to pinpoint since the triathlete can rarely feel the pain when not participating in exercise. Walking is usually pain-free. The injury is identified by nagging pain on the back of the upper leg. Usually the pain is deep-seated and difficult to isolate, although doing a hamstring stretch and running or cycling can bring on the painful feeling quickly.

A hamstring tear is usually caused either by overtraining or a biomechanical fault. It is generally the former that is to blame – the main culprit being a sudden increase in quality work training sessions.

Treatment

Since the injury is usually a deep-seated one, within the muscle, the best treatment is physiotherapy. The usual procedure involves cross-friction deep massage during which the muscle is encouraged to 'unknot' through a flexing, kneading and pressuring action over the area. This is intensely painful, though!

Often ultrasound treatment is an alternative method used to help with the healing.

As is the case with most injuries, prevention is better than cure. Strengthening of the hamstrings in the gym, under the guidance of a physiotherapist, is probably the best way of ensuring there won't be a reoccurrence.

8 THE WORLD'S GREAT RACES

Often the best way to judge the success of a sport is by the status of its flagship events. In the case of triathlon, the growth of a variety of international events and the success of some of the long-standing ones have demonstrated how successful the sport has become.

Triathlon perhaps owes much to US television network ABC, whose coverage from the mid-1980s on of the Hawaii Ironman World Championships has probably inspired more people to take up the sport than any other media form. Their presentation of Ironman as an event that can change lives – and in which anyone who finishes is a superstar – has made triathlon evolve into a sport to which everyone aspires.

The popularity of this ultra-distance event has spawned various genres of triathlon racing, the most recognized format being the Olympic Distance of a 1500m swim, 40km cycle and 10km run (0.9 mile; 25 miles; 6.2 miles).

So successful is this format that triathlon made its Olympic debut in Sydney, Australia, barely 12 years after it was first introduced. No other sport has ever gained Olympic recognition within this time frame.

Besides the Ironman and Olympic Distances, the success of Sprint Distance triathlons (usually half the length of an Olympic Distance event) has made the sport accessible to millions and continued to help develop fresh, young talent for the longer distances.

There are hundreds of races of varying distances in-between, however, with each offering the triathlete a different challenge. Probably the most exciting development in recent years has been the growth of off-road, or Xterra, triathlon. Starting with a swim, followed by an off-road mountain bike course and finishing with a cross-country run, this format poses fresh challenges and has revealed a new breed of Xterra specialists.

In the face of so many competing sports, triathlon has the potential to adapt better than most. Offering such a variety of options, the world's great races such as those featured in this chapter continue to be triathlon's lifeblood.

HAWAII IRONMAN

The big kahuna

It started in 1977 as an argument between a group of friends that included visionary US Navy officer John Collins – the debate was whether cyclists, swimmers or runners were the fittest. Collins proposed that the matter be decided by swimming the Waikiki Rough Water Swim, cycling the Oahu Round the Island Race and running the Honolulu Marathon course all in one stretch. The winner would be: the first Ironman. A small iron statue was made specially for the occasion.

Suffice to say, Collins' suggestion has spawned a million-dollar sporting enterprise and an event that every aspirant ultra-distance triathlete dreams of taking part in – despite the usually hot conditions in October, when the race takes place. Qualifying races for the Hawaii Ironman World Championships take place around the world, but entries are limited to just 1500 every year.

The course has now moved from Honolulu to Hawaii's Kona island. It takes in a 3.9km (2.4-mile) swim in pristine lagoon waters, a murderous and often windy 180km (112-mile) bike ride and an energy-sapping 42.2km (26.2-mile) marathon. Part of the success of the event has been the result of superb television coverage. NBC, which began covering the event in 1991, has won nine Emmy Awards for its unique perspective on the event.

LONDON OLYMPIC DISTANCE TRIATHLON

Big City Tri

In 2002, the London Triathlon attracted a capacity field of 2800 competitors all eager to, once a year, brave a triathlon for the sake of personal achievement and to raise money for others. Just like the London Marathon, the triathlon also has a strong charity function and thousands of pounds are raised each year when athletes get friends and colleagues to sponsor their race. Every August, thousands of spectators turn out to watch – excellent value for the sponsors.

Contrary to popular belief, the swim is not held in the polluted Thames River. Instead, the Royal Victoria Dock in London's Docklands district is the venue – here, the water meets European Union bathing standards as it is not tidal and the water is filtered.

The race is unique in that the transition area and finish take place indoors. Local star Simon Lessing is the most prolific winner; in 2002 he secured his sixth victory in a row.

In addition to the main event, there are also Sprint Distance events and relay formats. A recent innovation is a special sub-2-hour-30-minute age group race, or wave, that offers a special course for faster triathletes.

NICE ULTRA TRIATHLON

French fervour

Started in 1982, the 154km (95-mile) Nice triathlon is one of the oldest on the world calendar. This event attracts the best in the world: 11-time American champion Mark Allen, Dutch legend Rob Barel and Belgian Luc van Lierde have all been among the list of winners.

In a country passionate about anything involving bicycles, Nice is, despite its toughness, the most popular European long-distance event. Just 2000 competitors are able to enter each year to take on a course that starts with a long 4km (2.5-mile) swim along the coast, a tough 120km (74.5-mile) cycle that includes long climbs and sharp, technical descents and 30km (18.6-mile) of flat running along the scenic Promenade des Anglais. The event, held in September, is often used as the ITU World Long Distance Championships and attracts thousands of spectators. Mark Allen holds the course record of 05:46:10.

WILDFLOWER FESTIVAL

Triathlon's Woodstock

Held each May at Lake San Antonio, California, the Wildflower Festival is a three-day event that does for triathlon every year what Woodstock did for music. It is a major weekend of camping out, racing and socializing. Most of the people descending on Lake San Antonio normally are not there to race. It's a great social occasion that includes a series of triathlons, from off-road to Olympic, culminating in a tough Half Ironman. And the world's best triathletes are regular entries, as Wildflower is often regarded as an early test of one's form ahead of events like the Hawaii Ironman.

Australian legend Chris McCormack describes the main event 'as probably the toughest Half Ironman in the world' – and few would argue. The second half of the cycle course and the final 21.1km (13.1 miles) run are murderous.

Some 40,000 turn up for the festival, and since the nearest hotel is nearly 90km (50 miles) away, the only option for racers and student helpers alike is to camp. Luckily the racers are able to stay at a different area to the noisy students, who treat the weekend as one big party. In past events, one of the aid stations has even sported topless helpers!

LAGUNA PHUKET TRIATHLON

Thailand tri

It may not be the biggest triathlon in the world, but the Laguna Phuket event held in November each year has almost legendary status. Maybe it is the upmarket Laguna Phuket resort, which occupies 245ha (600 acres) of beachfront on the north-west coast of Thailand's Phuket island, that does the trick – or the presence of so many top international ultra- and short-distance athletes who have helped elevate the status of the race. Most likely it is the uniqueness of the course that draws entries from all over the world year after year.

The 1.8km (1-mile) swim is a two-leg affair: the first 1430m is swum in the sea and the last 370m in an adjacent lagoon (competitors run across 100m [330yd] of beach sand to get there). It is triathlon in its purist form and the 55km (34-mile) bike leg is a non-drafting event held on narrow twisting roads mingled with torturous climbs. The 12km (7.5-mile) running course is flatter but takes in a combination of paved roads, dirt trails and beach, and the potholes that competitors are warned to watch for. Conditions are typically hot and muggy, but it's worth the afterparty – which is a blast.

WORLD TRIATHLON EVENTS

Hawaii Ironman, USA

www.ironmantri.com

London Olympic Distance Triathlon, UK

www.thelondontriathlon.com

e-mail: info@thelondontriathlon.com

14-15 Lower Grosvenor Place, London SW1W OEX

• tel: +44-207-5592929 • fax: +44-207-5592849

Nice Ultra Triathlon, France

www.nice-triathlon.com

e-mail: fftri@fftri.com

Wildflower Festival, CA, USA

www.tricalifornia.com

e-mail: events@tricalifornia.com

Tri California, 1284 Adobe Lane, Pacific Grove, CA 93950

• tel: +1-831-3730678 • fax: +1-831-3737731

Laguna Phuket Triathlon, Thailand

www.lagunaphuket.com/triathlon/

e-mail: info@lagunaphuket.com

Laguna Resorts & Hotels, Bang Tao Beach, Phuket,Thailand

• tel: +66-76-324416/7 • fax: +66-76-324061

Xterra World Championships, USA

www.xterraplanet.com/race/

Xterra is a registered trademark of TEAM Unlimited, 500 Ala Moana Blvd., Two Waterfront Plaza, Suite 302, Honolulu, Hawaii, USA 96813

• tel: +1-808-5214322 • fax: +1-808-5380314

INTERNATIONAL TRIATHLON ORGANIZATIONS

Note: Websites for countries such as Italy, Netherlands, Czech Republic, Denmark, Finland, Norway and Sweden, appear in the relevant native language. Visit the website **www.triathlon.org** for information in English and direct links to these websites.

International Triathlon Union

www.triathlon.org; e-mail: ituhdq@triathlon.org

NORTH AMERICA

USA Triathlon

www.USATriathlon.org

e-mail: Info@USATriathlon.org

616 W Monument St., Colorado Springs, CO 80905

• tel: +1-719-5979090 • fax: +1-719-5972121

Triathlon Canada

www.triathloncanada.com

Info@TriathlonCanada.com

National Office, #606B, 1185 Eglinton Ave. E, Toronto, Ontario M3C 3C6

• tel: +1-416-4267180 • fax: +1-416-4267294

CENTRAL EUROPE

European Triathlon Union

www.triathlon.org/etu-website; www.etu-triathlon.org

British Triathlon Association

www.britishtriathlon.org

information@britishtriathlon.co.uk

Room 211, Sir John Beckwith Bdg., Loughborough University, Loughborough, Leicestershire LE11 3TU

• tel: +44-1509-226161 • fax: +44 1509-226165

German Triathlon Federation

Otto-Fleck-Schneise 12, 60528 Frankfurt / Main

• tel. +49-69-6772050 • fax: +49-69-67720511

SOUTHERN HEMISPHERE

Triathlon Australia

www.triathlon.org.au

e-mail: info@triathlon.org.au

20 Rodborough Rd., Frenchs Forest, NSW 2086

• tel: +61-2-99727999 • fax: +61-2-99727998

Triathlon New Zealand

www.triathlon.org.nz

e-mail: triathlonnz@xtra.co.nz

124 Bright St., Gisborne

• tel: +64-6-8633656 •fax: +64-6-8633657

Triathlon South Africa

www.triathlon.org/nf/southafrica/contact.htm

e-mail: topsport@mweb.co.za

Limomanis, 28 Viljoen St., Lydenburg 1120

• tel: +27-82-7895188 • fax: +27-13-2352608

TRIATHLON MAGAZINES

Triathlete Magazine (USA)

www.TriathleteMag.com

Triathlete Magazine (Germany)

www.triathlete-mag.de

Runner's World (South Africa)

(has won an award for its triathlon coverage)

www.runnersworld.co.za or visit www.runnersworld.com

INDEX

ACKNOWLEDGEMENTS

Without the input and assistance from the following people, this book would not have been possible. My thanks to Scott Tinley; Hazen Kent, Libby Burrell and LouAnn Rivett for their training programmes; Michael Yessis PHD, president of Sports Training Inc., California, USA, for his active stretch routine; Jane Downs for her help on the nutrition chapter; Wayne Viljoen for the weight-training advice; and to the many triathletes and coaches who have contributed to my knowledge of the sport. Special thanks to my wife and chief supporter, Janet, and my two sons, Wayde and Nicholas. Without them this book would never have been written!

The publishers would like to thank triathlete models Justin and Jason Berry, Claire Kinsley, Colin Williamson, Greg Goodall and Mike Maytham, who gave freely of their time and energy for our photo shoot.

PHOTOGRAPHIC CREDITS

All photography by Nicholas Aldridge for New Holland Image Library (NHIL), with the exception of the following photographers and/or their agencies (copyright rests with these individuals and/or their agencies).
[t = top; tc = top centre; tl = top left; tr = top right; b = bottom; bl = bottom left; br = bottom right]

Front Cover: Main picture: Rich Cruse tr=Gallo Images/gettyimages.com tc=Gallo Images/gettyimages.com

Page	Credit
2–3	Gallo Images/gettyimages.com
4–5	Sporting Pictures
6	Gallo Images/gettyimages.com
8–9	Gallo Images/gettyimages.com
10	Chilli/Allsport/Phil Cole
11	Rich Cruse
12	Hulton Getty
13	Touchline
14 tr	Rich Cruse
14 bl	Touchline
15	Touchline
16 tl	NHIL
16 bl	Gallo Images/gettyimages.com
17 tr	Imagebank
17 c	Imagebank
17 br	Photo Access
20	Gallo Images/gettyimages.com
21	Touchline
22	NHIL
23	Chilli/Allsport/Phil Cole
24	Gallo Images/gettyimages.com
28	Nigel Farrow
34	Imagebank
36 bl	NHIL
37 tr	NHIL
39	Touchline
42 tl	NHIL
42 bl	Gallo Images/gettyimages.com
43	NHIL
44	NHIL
45	NHIL
54	Masterfile
55	Imagebank
56	Touchline
58	Gallo Images/gettyimages.com
63	Touchline
65	Chilli/Allsport/Phil Cole
72 tl	NHIL
72 bl	Imagebank
73	Gallo Images/gettyimages.com
74–75	Gallo Images/gettyimages.com
76	NHIL
78	Chilli/Allsport/Phil Cole
80	Gallo Images/gettyimages.com
81	Chilli/Allsport/Phil Cole
84	Chilli/Allsport/Phil Cole
87	Touchline
88	Imagebank
92–93	Chilli/Allsport/Phil Cole
94	Chilli/Allsport/Phil Cole
98	Chilli/Allsport/Phil Cole
101	Rich Cruse
102	NHIL
103	NHIL
104 tr	NHIL
104 cr	NHIL
104 br	Gallo Images/gettyimages.com
105	NHIL
106	NHIL
107	NHIL
108	NHIL
109	NHIL
110	NHIL
111	Gallo Images/gettyimages.com
112	NHIL
115	Rich Cruse
116	Rich Cruse
117	Gallo Images/gettyimages.com
118	Digitaltriathlon
120	Chilli/Allsport/Phil Cole
124	Chilli/Allsport/Phil Cole
126 tl	Chilli/Allsport/Phil Cole
127	Chilli/Allsport/Phil Cole
128 bl	Chilli/Allsport/Phil Cole
129 tr	Touchline
129 br	Touchline
130	Rich Cruse
132	NHIL
133	NHIL
134	NHIL
135	Gallo Images/gettyimages.com
145	Gallo Images/gettyimages.com
146	Chilli/Allsport/Phil Cole
147	Gallo Images/gettyimages.com
148	Touchline
149	Touchline
150	AFP
151	Digitaltriathlon
152	AAP